Local Interest Politics

A One-Way Street

The Urban Governors Series

Local Interest Politics

A One-Way Street

Betty H. Zisk
Boston University

The Bobbs-Merrill Company, Inc. Indianapolis New York

Heinz Eulau, Stanford University
Kenneth Prewitt, University of Chicago

Coeditors, The Urban Governors Series

Printed in the United States of America
Library of Congress catalog card number 77–186245
First Printing
ISBN 0-672-51492-3

Editors' Preface

This study, like the others in *The Urban Governors* series, is based on data collected by the City Council Research Project, Institute of Political Studies, Stanford University. The CCRP was a collaborative research and research-training program made possible by grants from the National Science Foundation. Members of the project, all at one time or another doctoral candidates in political science at Stanford, were Betty H. Zisk, Boston University; Ronald O. Loveridge, University of California; Robert Eyestone, University of Minnesota; Peter A. Lupsha, Yale University; Thomas E. Cronin, University of North Carolina; Gordon Black, University of Rochester; Katherine Hinckley, Rice University; Stephen Ziony, City University of New York; Charles F. Levine, University of Illinois at Chicago Circle; and Helmut Kramer, Institute for Advanced Studies, Vienna. The editors served as principal and associate investigators, respectively.

Although the CCRP was centrally directed, each investigator contributed to the design of the research and was free to utilize the commonly collected data as he saw fit. Each monograph in this series therefore reflects the writer's own theoretical and substantive interests, and each writer is alone responsible for what he has written. Yet, the series as a whole is more than the sum of its parts. At the heart of the project was a concern with decision-making in small, natural-state legislative groups. Decisions coming out of city councils have far-reaching consequences for the lives of residents in a metropolitan region. While the project's central focus was on legislative behavior within the city council, topics as diverse as problems of metropolitan integration or the socialization and recruitment experiences of individual councilmen became matters of inquiry. As a result, the individual monographs in this series are variously linked not only to the literature on legislatures and representation, but also to the literature on urban government, policy outputs, elections, interest group politics, and other aspects of political life.

The "web of government" is complex, and its complexity makes for complex analysis. We solved the problem of complexity in the real world of politics by dividing the analytic labor among the project's members, and this is the reason that each volume in this series must stand on its own feet. But we would also insist that each volume contribute to the common enterprise of managing the complexity of political life without imposing on it any fashionable simple model of what politics is all about. In general, the units of analysis used in the different monographs are individual councilmen. A comprehensive study based on councils rather than on councilmen as units of analysis is also in preparation.

The major source of data was interviews conducted with 435 city councilmen in 87 cities of the greater San Francisco Bay region during 1966 and 1967. A description of the research site, research design, interview success, and related matters can be found in Appendix A. Some of the interviews were conducted by the members of the research team, but the bulk were undertaken by a group of professional interviewers including Jean J. Andrews, Sheryl Brown, Marion N. Fay, Helen M. Smelser, Sofia K. Thornburg, Mary E. Warren, and Betty E. Urquhart. Peter Lupsha served as field coordinator, Jean Stanislaw as research aide, and Virginia Anderson as project secretary. During the analytical phase of the project we have had the help of Sally Ferejohn as research assistant, Tex Hull as computer adviser, and Lois Renner as secretary.

Heinz Eulau
Kenneth Prewitt

Acknowledgments

A substantial intellectual debt is pending from the author to the two editors of this study, Heinz Eulau and Kenneth Prewitt. Over a period of eight years they have acted as friends, colleagues, and intellectual troubleshooters from the inception of the analysis, through the slow middle phase, to its completion. One might hope for such treatment from editors; it is delightful to receive such bounty from friends.

In addition, I am grateful for the help of a number of others. Stanley Zisk developed the original computer program to handle the data on which the study is based. Frances Burke and Harvey Boulay gave unstinting effort to the task of translating analytic afterthoughts into a computer-ready state. Lee Kane, Frances Burke, Harvey Boulay, and Edward Berger provided substantial critical advice during the final stages of writing. One of my sons, Stephen, acted as proofreading partner; my other two sons, Jonathan and Matthew, gave up many of their activities to provide the quiet needed to complete the work.

Finally, my thanks go to our sloop Éowyn, and to our Samoyeds, Il'ya and Jodie, for providing a vital change of pace on several occasions in the final stages of this work. It is not customary to dedicate a book to sailboats or dogs. If the author had more courage, however, she would devote one page to the phrase: "To Éowyn, Il'ya, and Jodie."

Contents

Appendixes

Tables

Figures and Maps

Chapter 1

Introduction

Nearly two centuries ago, the first analyst of American politics justified the proposed American constitution partially on the ground that it would help to control "the mischiefs of faction." Since James Madison wrote, the importance of factions—or of one modern equivalent, interest groups—has been treated as axiomatic by most observers of the American political system.[1] More recently, the assertion has been made that public policy can most fruitfully be viewed as the outcome of a "group struggle."[2]

To assert the importance of interest group activity is simple; to demonstrate influence in specific cases is not. One concludes, after studying the work of Lester Milbrath or Harry Eckstein, that group influence in both the United States and Britain is basically a residual category, operative only after all other factors have been taken into account by the legislator.[3] We read with a sense of anticlimax Bertram Gross's admission that he has, after all,

---

1 While Madison was probably referring to political parties, his definition of factions as "a number of citizens . . . who are united and actuated *by some common impulse of passion, or of interest* adverse to the rights of other citizens, or to the permanent and aggregate interest of the community" (emphasis added) provides a justification for considering modern interest groups as functional equivalents to parties.

2 See, for example, Bertram M. Gross, *The Legislative Struggle: A Study in Social Combat* (New York: McGraw-Hill Book Company, 1953).

3 Lester W. Milbrath, *The Washington Lobbyists* (Chicago: Rand McNally, 1963), and Harry Eckstein, *Pressure Group Politics: The Case of the British Medical Association* (Stanford: Stanford University Press, 1960).

been unable to document a single instance where group pressures changed a single vote.[4] And if the work of Richard Dawson and James Robinson, Thomas Dye, Richard Hofferbert, and others has convincingly demonstrated that neither party competition nor citizen participation is a major determinant of fiscal policy, one wonders what role, if any, interest groups play in the formation of public policy.[5]

Why, if this is all we have learned, have we followed the peregrinations and machinations of these groups with such avid attention? Why the polemics and the monographs on a subject so elusive, and perhaps so insignificant? We might consider several explanations. Perhaps the observers and analysts of group activity have assumed an ability to influence where there is in fact none. Alternatively, the question of group influence may be, like the concepts of "freedom" and "justice," not readily susceptible to empirical treatment. Finally, it is possible that explanations for "influence" have been sought in the wrong places. Research emphasis on internal organization, cohesion, and tactics of interest groups may have told only part of the story.

The project described in the pages that follow is based on a provisional acceptance of the third alternative. We assume that any attempt to analyze influence must take into account the behavior and biases of all major parties to the transaction observed. While most analysts of group activity have stated their general acceptance of this viewpoint, very few studies have focused on the predispositions *of legislators* toward group activity.[6] This omis-

---

[4] Gross, *The Legislative Struggle,* pp. 388–389.

[5] See, for example, Richard E. Dawson and James A. Robinson, "Inter-Party Competition, Economic Variables and Welfare Policies in the American States," *Journal of Politics* 25 (1963): 265–289; Thomas R. Dye, *Politics, Economics and the Public* (Chicago: Rand McNally, 1966); and Richard I. Hofferbert, "The Relation Between Public Policy and Some Structural and Environmental Variables in the American States," *American Political Science Review* 60 (1966): 73–82. A comprehensive review and critique of the input-output literature is found in Herbert Jacob and Michael Lipsky, "Outputs, Structure, and Power: An Assessment of Changes in the Study of State and Local Politics," *Journal of Politics* 30 (1968): 510–538.

[6] The major exceptions to this comment are Wahlke's study of state legislator-interest group relations in John C. Wahlke et al., *The Legislative System:*

sion is a serious one, for a focus on legislative predispositions may help to specify the conditions under which interest group efforts to influence public policy will or will not meet with success.

We might account for influence by two general propositions:

1. The predispositions of elected officials will act as a filter through which group efforts to influence public policy must pass. How accessible officials are to groups will depend in part on these predispositions.
2. Given the predispositions of elected officials not only toward interest groups but toward other important actors in the political system (political parties, administrators, fellow legislators), the influence of specific groups will vary with internal group organization, tactical skills, and cohesion.

The bulk of previous study has been confined to the second statement. We shall focus on hypotheses related to the first of these propositions in order to supplement existing work.

Context of the Study

The data used for this study were obtained through interviews with one near-total universe of legislators: city councilmen in 82 of the 89 cities of the San Francisco Bay Area.[7] Our study of councilman/interest group relations is one part of a larger project

---

Explorations in Legislative Behavior (New York: John Wiley and Sons, 1962); Oliver Garceau and Corinne Silverman, "A Pressure Group and the Pressured," *American Political Science Review* 48 (1954); and Harmon Zeigler and Michael Baer, *Lobbying: Interaction and Influence in American State Legislatures* (Belmont, Calif.: Wadsworth Publishing Company, 1969).

[7] Data were collected from 435 councilmen in 87 cities (see Appendix A, p. 162), and all responses to questions cited in the following analysis are included in our tabulations. We refer to *82 cities,* however, in most of our study, because in five of the 87 cities either only a minority of councilmen were interviewed (3 cities) or only a minority answered the questions upon which the typology of interest group orientations was based (2 cities). One additional city was omitted from the analysis in Chapter 7 because less than a majority answered the questions on which our measures of group activity were based.

comparing several aspects of the behavior of actors in small legislative systems. Interviews and self-administered questionnaires covered a wide range of topics, including recruitment of councilmen, relations between councilmen and political parties, groups, city staff, and community influentials, and formal and informal relations within the council itself. Interview data were supplemented by records of local expenditures, land use, population characteristics, and voting results over a period of years. The major characteristics of the San Francisco Bay Area and of the City Council Research Project are described in detail in Appendix A, together with methods of data collection, processing, and analysis.

Many of the propositions implied or asserted in current descriptions of local government date back to the reform ideology of the Progressive movement and to recommendations made in the wake of early twentieth-century exposures of corruption in city government by muckrakers like Lincoln Steffens. Few of the assertions of those advocating nonpartisanship in local elections or the employment of a city manager have been subjected to even the crudest empirical testing. The little empirical research that does exist was undertaken primarily by (1) students of public administration, through case studies that focus on unique decisions or controversies and pay little or no attention to the theoretical relevance of the findings; (2) sociologists interested in the structure of community power, whose research has been conducted largely without reference to formal institutions like city councils; and (3) psychologists and sociologists interested in questions such as the correlates of adult participation in voluntary associations, the incidence of *anomie* and alienation (or of the opposite, "moral integration"), again with little attention to the formal structure of decision-making.[8]

As recently as 1957, Lawrence Herson wrote that the study of city government—"lacking, for example, its first comparative study

---

[8] With the recent resurgence of scholarly interest in urban politics, it is to be hoped that this comment will soon need modification. For a representative collection of urban studies spanning the years 1889 to 1968, see Edward C. Banfield, ed., *Urban Government: A Reader in Administration and Politics* (rev. ed.; New York: The Free Press, 1969).

of the city council—has yet to amass much . . . necessary knowledge."[9] Since then, a number of suggestive studies have been undertaken in Los Angeles, Milwaukee, Philadelphia, and elsewhere.[10] Yet there is still little systematic knowledge of the bases upon which local officials make decisions or of the way in which they relate to significant actors in the community.

A similar hiatus exists in regard to the study of local interest groups. An impressive number of studies have been made of the efforts by interest groups to influence Congress, the Executive, and state legislatures. Very little study has been devoted to the relations between group spokesmen and members of urban decision-making bodies. It is possible that organizations such as manufacturers associations, labor unions, and spokesmen for minority groups believe they have little or no stake in the decisions of city councils, school boards, and other community bodies. It is further possible that at the community level some or most "private" groups lose their identity as advocates for a particular interest because they are co-opted by official policy-makers as administrative agents for local government.[11] However, there is almost no systematic evidence to answer these empirical questions.

Part of our task is thus to distinguish the conditions under which:

1. interest groups are aloof from the arena of local politics;

---

[9] Lawrence J. R. Herson, "The Lost World of Municipal Government," *American Political Science Review* 51 (1957): 340.

[10] Robert J. Huckshorn and Charles E. Young, "Study of Voting Splits on City Councils in Los Angeles County," *Western Political Quarterly* 13 (1960): 479–497; Henry Schmandt, "The City and the Ring," *The American Behavioral Scientist* 4 (1960): 17–19; Gladys Kammerer et al., *City Managers in Politics: An Analysis of Manager Tenure and Termination* (Gainesville: University of Florida Press, 1962); Oliver P. Williams, Harold Herman, Charles S. Liebman, and Thomas R. Dye, *Suburban Differences and Metropolitan Policies: A Philadelphia Story* (Philadelphia: University of Pennsylvania Press, 1965).

[11] For examples of this phenomenon, see Morton Grodzins, "Local Strength in the American Federal System: The Mobilization of Public-Private Influence," in Marian D. Irish, ed., *Continuing Crisis in American Politics* (Englewood Cliffs, N.J.: Prentice-Hall, 1963), pp. 132–152.

2. interest groups are active advocates or contenders for community resources, and
   a. become partners in some aspect of the policy-making process itself; or
   b. become adversaries to the major policy-making bodies in the community.

We cannot assume that a model of "group struggle" is useful or even applicable to local government until we have some idea of what groups are active in local politics and under what conditions their activity can become an important determinant of policy.

Nevertheless, our primary interest is neither in the way in which local decisions are made by local officials, nor in the manner in which community interest groups differ from their equivalents in state or national politics. We are concerned instead with answering some questions about how interests are voiced and *with what effect* in American political systems. What impact do group demands have on policy outputs? on the relations between policy-makers and other significant actors in local communities?

The main contribution of such a study consists in identifying uniformities in political behavior through a comparison of similar phenomena in a wide variety of political settings. The choice of a research site where officials are reasonably accessible and the units of analysis are manageable facilitates this aim. City councils in the San Francisco Bay Area range (with one exception) from five to nine members. It is therefore possible to interview a relatively small number of councilmen and then make valid statements about a relatively large number of separate units.

Limits of the Study

Several questions arise concerning the nature of the inferences which can be made on the basis of data obtained from interviews with one set of actors in small nonpartisan political systems. Can statements be made which apply to actors in political systems at the state or federal level? Do conclusions apply to systems where elections are partisan? What is the relation between the "reality" perceived by councilmen and the "reality" that might be described by other actors (e.g., interest group spokesmen), or that inferred by research into documentary sources?

The question of the validity of inferences from one level of politics to another is one of the most difficult methodological problems confronting those who study political behavior. However, let us make two assumptions: (1) that the human actors in all political systems will behave at least partially in accordance with the expectations of others; and (2) that the tasks performed by political systems in order to function as systems involve individuals taking certain roles in some structure that is part of the system. We are then justified in inferring that *patterns* found in local politics probably have their equivalent in state or national politics. Our ability to make such inferences depends largely upon the level of abstraction of the theory tested. For this reason, a structural-functional approach is combined here with role analysis in dealing with the predispositions of councilmen toward interest groups.

Most studies of interest group activity have been based on observations of interest groups in action or upon interviews with group leaders. We have, in contrast, relied upon the perceptions and reported behavior of councilmen as regards local interest groups.

There is dual justification for the choice of the councilman's perceptual world as the "reality" relevant to the present problem. First, the main question to be asked concerns the implications of *councilmen's* predispositions for the effectiveness of interest group activity. Second, there is no reason to assume a priori that other research techniques (e.g., interviews with interest group spokesmen) would yield substantially different or qualitatively better information.

For example, we may have reason to believe that spokesmen for local business organizations are substantially more accurate in presenting members' views, by whatever standard we select, than are local union officials. Still, we cannot assume that this difference affects the influence of the two organizations unless we know that the difference is both perceived and considered important by city councilmen.

One fruitful approach to the question would therefore seem to be to ascertain and rely on the views of the councilman himself—in short, to follow the suggestion of W. I. Thomas that the actor's "definition of the situation" is the relevant datum.[12] This is not to suggest that the method followed here can supplant methods relying on other "realities." Rather, our position is that different approaches should yield complimentary information.

A closely allied question remains. Some earlier studies of the predispositions of legislators have been criticized for failing to link attitudes to concrete behavior.[13] Indeed, this problem is not confined to the study of legislative behavior; it must also be reckoned with by students of voting behavior, political socialization, and a host of other topics that have relied on the attitude survey. We take the criticism seriously.

Consequently, our own position rests on three points. First, we shall utilize information provided by councilmen on their concrete activity as well as their attitudes and perceptions. This data should provide a check on the link between predispositions and acts. Second, we find no overriding reason to prefer the reports of newspapermen or others to councilmen's information on their own behavior. Finally, we assume at least a minimal "strain toward consistency" on the part of political actors, i.e., some effort to bring attitudes and acts into a reasonable degree of harmony.[14] Given some independent evidence about those acts, we will have an opportunity to check the accuracy of this final assumption.

---

[12] See Edmund I. Volkart, ed., *Social Behavior and Personality: Contributions of W. I. Thomas to Theory and Social Research* (New York: Social Science Research Council, 1951), "Introduction," for a discussion of this viewpoint.

[13] See, for example, Wayne L. Francis, "The Role Concept in Legislatures: A Probability Model and a Note on Cognitive Structure," *Journal of Politics* 27 (1965): 568, and Zeigler and Baer, *Lobbying,* p. 152.

[14] A great deal of effort has been devoted over the last decades to the study of "cognitive balance" and "cognitive dissonance." See, for example, Leon Festinger, *A Theory of Cognitive Dissonance* (Evanston, Ill.: Row, Peterson and Co., 1957).

Outline of the Analysis

We begin in the next chapter with a brief description of our approach to the study of local interest politics and the typology of councilmen's group role orientations used in this study. Chapters 3 through 6 present and analyze the relevant data, moving from the attitudes and perceptions of councilmen to the antecedents and consequences of their behavior.

In Chapter 7 we shift from the analysis of individual behavior to a study of councilmen/interest group relations on a city-by-city basis. Here the effort is made to relate council/group relations to the economic and social environment on the one hand, and to policy outcomes on the other. Chapter 8 concludes our study with a discussion of the theoretical and research applications of these findings.

Chapter 2

Local Interest Politics: An Overview

Some years ago, Samuel Eldersveld classified studies of American interest groups into three types: case studies; studies of interest group activity in a single arena (especially the legislative); and the study of group activities related to a particular law or policy conflict.[1] Insofar as the present work falls into any of Eldersveld's three categories, it clearly belongs with the second: the study of groups operating within a single arena.

Most studies of this type have been based on an implicit model of the legislator as a passive recipient of "outside" pressures. As Harry Eckstein put it, the legislator simply served as a cash register, ringing up claims and debits as they were entered by parties, pressure groups, and all those who could mobilize support outside the legislature.[2] David Truman used the analogy of the steel ball in the pinball machine to criticize this implicit model,[3] while Wahlke referred to the assumption as a "parallelogram-of-forces model of pressure politics and legislative behavior."[4]

---

1 Samuel J. Eldersveld, "American Interest Groups: A Survey of Research and Some Implications for Theory and Method," in Henry W. Ehrmann, ed., *Interest Groups on Four Continents* (Pittsburgh: University of Pittsburgh Press, 1958), p. 175.

2 Eckstein, *Pressure Group Politics,* p. 153.

3 David Truman, *The Governmental Process* (New York: Alfred A. Knopf, 1951), pp. 332–333.

4 John C. Wahlke et al., "American State Legislators' Role Orientations Toward Pressure Groups," *Journal of Politics* 22 (1960): 204.

The assumption that legislators are passive recipients of outside pressures led to a research emphasis on problems of internal organization, leadership skills, and group strategy—characteristics believed to be crucial to "access" and "influence." What was left out of the picture were the predispositions of the legislators, the screen through which all group efforts had to pass.

However, even after the weaknesses of the parallelogram-of-forces model were recognized and students of interest group activity began to take into account variables such as the legislators' group affiliations,[5] few attempts were made to develop another model that would systematically relate all variables relevant to the complex relations between members of interest groups and official bodies. In 1950, Stephen Bailey proposed a vector model consisting of Pendleton Herring's "four I's" (institutions, ideas, interests and individuals) that would encompass both interest group and legislative activity. Yet he failed to develop the model to the point where it was operational for even his own research purposes.[6]

In the last two decades, students of interest groups have adopted a wide variety of theoretical orientations. (See Appendix B for a brief discussion of both interest group studies and works on local politics relevant to the present study.) Our own work is most indebted to the analysis by John Wahlke, Heinz Eulau, William Buchanan, and Leroy Ferguson of the legislative system in four American states.[7]

The Wahlke study begins with the premise that state legislatures and other organizations and individuals concerned with making

---

[5] See, for example, Ralph K. Huitt, "The Congressional Committee: A Case Study," *American Political Science Review* 48 (1954): 340–365, and Charles R. Jones, "Representation in Congress: The Case of the House Agricultural Committee," *American Political Science Review* 55 (1961): 358–367.

[6] Stephen K. Bailey, *Congress Makes a Law: The Story Behind the Employment Act of 1946* (New York: Columbia University Press, 1950), "Preface," p. x.

[7] Wahlke et al., *The Legislative System*. One precursor of the interest group portion of the Wahlke study was the *American Political Science Review* article by Garceau and Silverman, "A Pressure Group and the Pressured." Garceau and Silverman developed a general typology of role orientations toward the legislative process, but they did not study roles played by legislators in regard to specific sets of actors, e.g., party leaders, constituents, etc., as did Wahlke.

public decisions can be viewed as legislative systems. This system consists of interdependent sets of actors (e.g., legislators, interest group leaders, party officials, constituents) who play roles in accordance with mutual expectations. The function of the system is to transform inputs (demands and supports) into political outputs (laws and rulings allocating resources). The advantage of this approach is its ability to relate individual actors to institutional arrangements and to take into account, simultaneously, informal norms and formal legal enactments. It links such disparate subjects as legislator/interest group relations, social status, friendship patterns, and bloc or party membership of legislators, without drawing on concepts extraneous to the initial formulation.

Because it deals with small legislative systems in a nonpartisan setting, the present study has supplemented the role analysis-systems approach with a specification of inputs and outputs that do not rely exclusively on traditional institutions studied in the United States (e.g., political parties). It is likely, given the legal provisions regarding local elections in California, that parties play a very minor role in the local political system. Furthermore, there is no reason to assume interest groups are the only, or even the major, means through which constituents make claims on public officials. Several studies of politics in the local community[8] give the impression that highly personalized political relations in small or moderate-sized communities may eliminate the need for intensive interest group activity.

We are thus led to ask not only what functions community interest groups perform as part of a local legislative system but also to inquire what other formal or informal means there are for the expression of demands or claims on community resources. Not only are we interested in the way in which public claims are articulated and processed in local political systems, but we are also concerned with the *consequences* of this process.

If, for example, access to officials is granted to interest groups in direct proportion to group "cohesion,"[9] do the interests of such

---

[8] For example, Arthur J. Vidich and Joseph Bensman, *Small Town in Mass Society* (New York: Doubleday, 1958).

[9] Truman, *The Governmental Process,* especially Chapter 11.

relatively uncohesive and unorganized groups as consumers or the unemployed go ignored by political decision-makers? Or do alternative means exist for the expression of such interests? What are the long-run consequences for the community and its citizens of different means of presenting claims? Our initial inquiry thus poses a set of three questions:

1. How is interest group activity perceived by public officials, and how receptive are they to such activity?
2. How and why do officials differ in their perceptions and attitudes toward interest group activity?
3. What are the implications of such differences for the political system?

Preliminary Remarks on City Councils as Role Systems

To analyze the interest group/city councilman relationship, we utilize the idea of a role system linking councilmen to all other actors concerned with the policy-making process in the local community. We assume that each councilman can play a number of roles with respect to several "significant others": his fellow councilmen, the city staff, his constituents, interest groups, political parties, and members of other decision-making bodies. We may view the relationship between the councilman and each of these sets of actors as "role sectors" (e.g., his role toward interest groups may be termed an interest group role relevant to the interest articulation sector). The way in which a given role is played will be to some degree limited for the actor, both by formal rules (perhaps all interest groups are legally granted the right to appear at public hearings) and by informal norms (perhaps the belief is common that "all groups have a right to be heard"). In addition, the role expectations of members of interest groups themselves may be important. These expectations may be backed by sanctions of varying effectiveness. A large group that is denied access may be able to mobilize enough electoral strength to defeat council incumbents. A small group may be reduced to back-fence complaining. At the same time, an actor probably will have considerable choice within these limits. For example, without encountering strong sanctions, he may take either an active and encouraging role or a neutral role toward groups. Under some circumstances, depending on the community he represents, he may be able to take a negative role.

An actor's role orientation in a given role sector has implications for other role sectors as well. If the actor is primarily concerned with the internal cohesion of the council itself, and one of the shared council norms is a refusal to accommodate groups, his group role orientation will be circumscribed by his council role orientation. If his constituency role includes the style of Trustee (a legislator who relies primarily on his own convictions rather than instructions for making decisions), his accessibility to interest articulation structures will in all probability be limited. Extreme caution must be exercised in assuming a consistency of roles for each actor. We may postulate a "strain toward consistency" but discover apparent contradictions. An actor's own sense of consistency may be maintained through "misperceptions" depending in part on his reference groups and in part on his capacity for rationalization and compartmentalization. Actors may vary in their tolerance of inconsistency. Finally, the expectations of others in the system may be either unclear or contradictory. In short, the degree of perceived inconsistency depends largely on the actor's own definition of the situation.[10]

We may observe a given actor who simultaneously assumes the role of Trustee, articulates the interests of organized labor at the council table, and agrees with his fellow council members that "having an axe to grind" is a violation by a councilman of the

---

[10] This viewpoint is the basis for a substantial body of theory and research on individual personality and small groups. It is based on the theoretical formulations of Kurt Lewin. See especially his *Field Theory in Social Science* (New York: Harper and Brothers, 1951). Field theory was considered as a basis for the present study, since the perspective seems particularly appropriate to the present problem. A whole range of variables, both internal and external, can be handled as "vectors" causing individual "locomotion" in a field (changes in previous states, whether cognitive, affective, or behavioral). The major drawback of the approach is the difficulty of making it operational for research dealing with complex systems.

"rules of the game." To explain these apparent inconsistencies, the outside observer must ask, among other things: (1) whether organized labor is an important reference group for this councilman and if he is sensitive primarily to cues from that group, and (2) whether he fails to perceive a conflict between his desire to contribute to council cohesion and his own role as spokesman for labor. If the answer to both questions is yes, then from his perspective there is no intrapersonal role conflict: he can serve his conscience since he is not knowingly undermining council cohesion. There is probably a conflict between his role orientation and the counterexpectations of others, unless the political system in question is dominated by union members and their families. In the latter case, the wishes of labor may have become institutionalized as community norms.

The point that role conflict can only be established on the basis of knowledge of mutual perceptions and expectations may seem obvious. It is important, however, to note two implications: (1) while correlations between, for example, interest group roles and representational roles taken by all councilmen in several systems may be informative in regard to the internal consistency of role systems, they must be supplemented by a comparative knowledge of specific communities; and (2) an important element in role orientations of actors is their view of the boundaries of the system. In the example just given, if the councilman in question is not from a predominantly union-member constituency, he may be oriented to a reference group (unions) not considered relevant to the system by other councilmen or by his own constituents. From the point of view of his fellow actors, he would then be adopting a role influenced by others who are external to the system; from his own viewpoint, his fellow actors would be ignoring an important part of the system.

Morris Janowitz has called suburbs "communities of limited liability."[11] One implication of this phrase is that the range of possible activities of decision-making bodies in such communities is limited in such a way that a large number of possible role

---

[11] Morris Janowitz, *The Community Press in an Urban Setting* (New York: The Free Press, 1952), Chapter 7.

relationships are not relevant. This statement is of course true for all political systems. There are a number of roles (e.g., family roles) that have little or no bearing on the political system. But if a community political system exists to deal with a narrow range of problems, the maintenance of boundaries becomes important for the functioning of that system. Disagreement over boundaries (or the relevance of some possible role relationships) may be a major source of conflict. Such disagreements affect the way in which cities handle metropolitan problems, since proposed solutions may be balanced against shared community norms in different ways by different sets of actors in the community. This carries obvious implications regarding both system stability and adaptation.

A Definition of Terms

Definitions of key terms utilized in the above discussion and in later chapters will be helpful at this point.

The term *role,* as used in this study, follows the prior usage of Wahlke and associates, which in turn draws largely upon the work of Theodore Newcomb.[12] A role is a set of "norms" or "expectations" of behavior supposed to apply to a given position (in this instance, that of councilman) by those involved in the transactions observed. No assumption is made that these expectations are uniformly shared. In fact, our earlier discussion has posed several instances where counterexpectations may arise to bring about role conflict.[13]

The term *role orientation* has been borrowed from Eulau:

> Role orientations are legislators' own expectations of the kind of behavior they ought to exhibit in the performance of their duties. They may be considered as providing the premises in terms of which legislators make decisions.[14]

---

[12] See Wahlke et al., *The Legislative System,* especially pp. 8–9, and Theodore M. Newcomb, *Social Psychology* (New York: The Dryden Press, 1950), Chapter 9.

[13] Neal Gross et al., *Explorations in Role Analysis* (New York: John Wiley & Sons, 1958), pp. 73–74.

[14] In Wahlke et al., *The Legislative System,* pp. 73–74.

The term *system* refers to a network of role relationships that may be viewed as performing interrelated input and output functions. A *political system* is a network of role relationships involving the authoritative allocation of limited resources.[15]

Included in the local political system are all of the actors concerned with this allocation process. It is possible to designate different sets of actors as those concerned primarily with "interest articulation," "recruitment," or other such functions; however, in the small and informal political systems with which we are concerned, a given set of actors may alternate between input and output roles, or even take both roles simultaneously. For example, members of the Chamber of Commerce may at one time perform interest articulation functions—by asking the council for a change in zoning ordinances to attract new business to the city; at another or the same time they may concern themselves with administrative functions—by carrying on a public relations campaign for the city at the request of the council. Or a councilman may act simultaneously as a legislator on behalf of the community and as an interest articulator within the council.

The main elements entering into role orientations, from the perspective of the individual actor, are shown in Figure 2–1. A role orientation is conditioned by the actor's previous experiences, the community environment, and the current expectations of significant others within the political system. The actor's role behavior, based on his role orientations, is the link between political inputs (claims and supports of the system) and political outputs (laws and other decisions).

It might be noted that the political system under consideration

---

[15] The word "resources" as used here applies to both tangibles (e.g., distribution of tax resources, decisions regarding land use) and intangibles (e.g., distribution of benefits involving status or respect without necessarily involving tangible items, such as appointment to honorary or ceremonial positions). Considerable attention has been devoted by political scientists during the past few decades to a search for an all-purpose definition of the words "politics" and "political"—see, for example, David Easton, *The Political System* (New York: Alfred A. Knopf, 1953), for a sensitive appraisal of some efforts in this direction. The above definition, which is similar to Easton's "authoritative allocation of values," and like Easton's is derived from the Parsonian framework, is simply an effort to find a *working* definition for purposes of this study.

Figure 2–1
Elements in Role Orientations
of City Councilman "A"

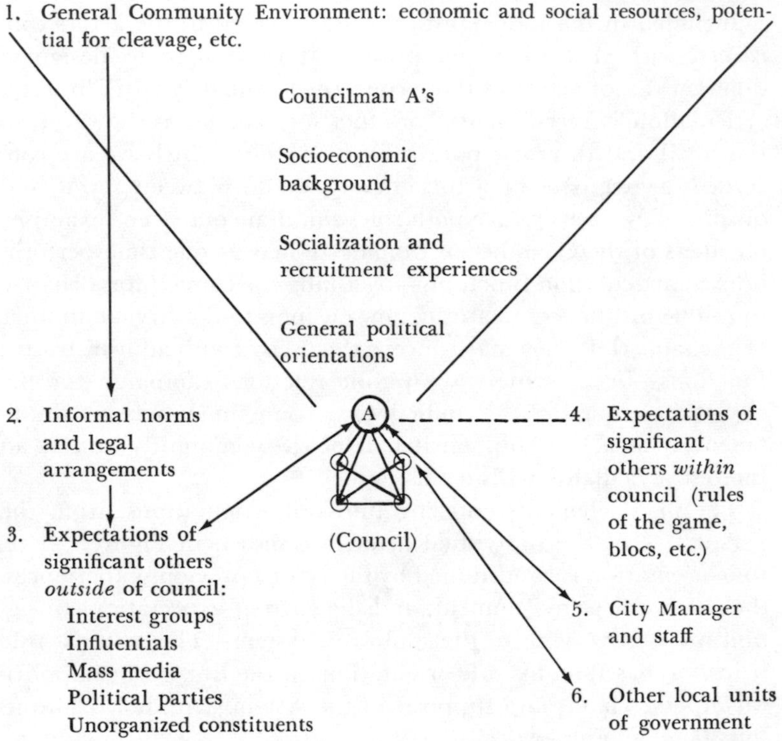

1. General Community Environment: economic and social resources, potential for cleavage, etc.

Councilman A's

Socioeconomic background

Socialization and recruitment experiences

General political orientations

2. Informal norms and legal arrangements

3. Expectations of significant others *outside* of council:
   Interest groups
   Influentials
   Mass media
   Political parties
   Unorganized constituents

A

(Council)

4. Expectations of significant others *within* council (rules of the game, blocs, etc.)

5. City Manager and staff

6. Other local units of government

might be studied by a variety of research techniques. Inputs might be measured by observation of contacts between councilmen and "significant others," by observation of interactions between councilmen and others at council hearings, or through a sampling of councilmen's mail. Similarly, outputs could be studied by an analysis of public decisions made by councilmen. In the present study, the research foci are: (1) the clientele role orientations of councilmen and, in particular, the interest group role orientation; and (2) the representational styles and purposive role orientations of councilmen. Information about these orientations—and the patterns of behavior associated with them—is obtained through interviews with the councilmen themselves.

A Typology of Role Orientations

The main analytical tool for this study is a typology of councilmen's role orientations toward interest groups. This typology is constructed on the basis of three variables: councilmen's attitudes toward interest groups; the extent to which "influential" groups are perceived; and level of "sophistication" with regard to the group universe. This typology is used to account for some of the differences in the accessibility of councilmen to groups and variations in their willingness to accommodate group requests. Further, it is related to councilmen's backgrounds and to their orientations toward other role sectors in the political system.

On the basis of the three variables listed in the preceding paragraph, three types of councilmen can be distinguished:

1. *Pluralists*: those who esteem groups, who perceive many groups, and who are relatively sophisticated in regard to the group universe.
2. *Tolerants*: a. those who are neutral toward groups, regardless of perception or group sophistication;
   b. those who esteem or reject groups, but demonstrate both a low level of perception and group sophistication;
   c. those who esteem groups, but are either "unsophisticated" or "low" perceivers.
3. *Antagonists*: those who reject groups and demonstrate high perception and/or group sophistication.

See Appendix C for a detailed description of the construction of this typology and the distribution of our respondents.

We use the typology to account for differences in the attitudes and behavior of councilmen toward local groups. Contrasting role orientations imply differences in the willingness of councilmen to accommodate group requests, quite apart from differential treatment that may hinge on the characteristics of the groups themselves. Differing group role orientations may also be associated with a parallel set of orientations toward other interest articulation agencies in the community: influential individuals, the press, and political parties. And the policy decisions of a council where the Pluralist orientation is dominant will probably differ substantially from those of an Antagonist-dominated or Tolerant-dominated council.

It is desirable to trace insofar as possible the antecedents of differing group role orientations. Particularly important in this respect are the economic and social characteristics of the communities in which the councilmen operate, and the general patterns of recruitment for public office in their cities. The choice of a specific role orientation may hinge in large part on the unique experiences and predilections of individual councilmen. We anticipate, nevertheless, systematic differences in the choice of such orientations—differences dependent upon the economic and social complexity of the urban or suburban environment, the quality of group life in the community, and the shared norms regarding appropriate means for attaining public office and appropriate behavior once that office is attained.

Chapter 3

Councilmen's Views and Relations with Community Interest Groups

The task of this chapter is threefold: first, to describe "group life," as perceived by city councilmen in 82 Bay Area cities; second, to examine the relation between the perceptions, attitudes, and behavior of these councilmen toward community interest groups; and finally, to construct a typology of councilmen's interest group role orientations. This typology will be utilized in the remainder of the study to account for differing attitudes and behavior toward both formal groups and alternative interest articulation structures, and toward other aspects of the political process in the cities studied.

It should be emphasized that the present undertaking is a description and analysis of the local "group struggle" *as perceived by one set of actors in the local political system.*[1] When statements are made about the intensity or nature of group life in Bay Area cities, it should be remembered that the group life under discussion is that perceived by the councilmen, whether or not a qualifying statement to this effect is included.

[1] See Introduction and Appendix A for a more detailed discussion of the methodological and theoretical implications of employing these kinds of data.

Group Life in 82 Cities

Perceptions of Groups in the Community

The councilmen were asked a variety of questions about interest groups in their communities in order to ascertain the quantity and quality of group activities they perceive: How many groups are active? What do these groups *do* to bring claims into the political system? How effective are these group activities?

As can be seen from Table 3–1, an overwhelming majority of councilmen believe that at least one group is "influential" on issues coming before the council.[2] Only a bare majority, however, name more than two influential organizations. The most frequent choice is the local Chamber of Commerce—perceived as influential by about two-thirds of the councilmen and accounting for one-quarter of the total mentioned. General civic organizations (service clubs, PTAs, the League of Women Voters) comprise almost one-third of the groups named. Finally, homeowners groups and neighborhood associations account for an additional 17 percent. Surprisingly, in contrast to these general civic and economic organiza-

Table 3–1
Number of Groups Perceived as Influential

Number of Groups Named	Percentage of Respondents (N = 431)	Cumulative Percentage
0	16	16
1	16	32
2	17	49
3	18	67
4	16	83
5 or more	17	100
	100	

[2] The question was: "Speaking of groups or organizations here in (city) which are active in community affairs and sometimes appear before the council—which would you say are the most influential?" Up to five groups were coded for each respondent.

Table 3–2
Types of Organizations Named as Influential
by 362 Respondents

Type of Organization	Times Mentioned	Total Responses*
General Economic Groups:		
Chamber of Commerce, Jaycees	273	
Neighborhood groups, homeowners associations, taxpayers groups	172	
	445	43%
General Civic Groups:		
Service clubs	121	
Women's organizations (League of Women Voters, American Association of University Women, PTA)	101	
Church groups	16	
Press	12	
Miscellaneous (youth-oriented, cultural, etc.)	60	
	310	31
Special Interests:		
Merchants associations	82	
Conservation groups	30	
Realtors associations	27	
Civil rights groups	19	
Builders and developers	14	
Veterans groups	14	
Unions	13	
Party clubs and organizations	10	
Senior citizens	8	
Farmers organizations	5	
"Right wing" groups	4	
	226	23
Semi-Official and Official Bodies:		
Planning Commission, Citizens Advisory Committees, School Committee, County Commissions	25	2
Total	1006	100%

* Up to four organizations were coded for each respondent. Thus the additional one or two groups named by the 68 councilmen who named five or more groups are not included in this tabulation.

tions, business, labor, and other spokesmen for special interests (conservationists, civil rights groups, veterans, etc.) are named infrequently. Table 3–2 presents this information in summary form.

A subject of some theoretical interest is the concentration or dispersion of influence among community groups. If most of the incumbents of the same city council attribute influence to the same handful of groups, we can probably infer an interlocking and homogeneous activist milieu for that city. At the other extreme, we might find communities where each councilman names a different set of organizations for whom he performs brokerage tasks or to whom he turns for advice and support. Differing patterns of influence will be examined at a later point in this study. For the present, a brief resume is presented in Table 3–3. The number of different "influential groups" per city ranged from none in four cities, to 21 in one large, economically diverse university city where there were nine respondents. As can be seen from the table, seven or more different groups were named in just over half of the 82 cities.

Another possible measure of the concentration or dispersion of influence is the number of groups that a *majority* of incumbents perceive as "influential." We find in about 20 percent of the cities, that no groups are agreed upon; in about 60 percent of the cities one or two groups are named by a majority; and in the remaining

Table 3–3
Number of Different Influential Groups Named
in 82 Cities

Number of Different Groups Named	Percentage of Cities
0	5
1–4	23
5–6	20
7–9	24
10–13	20
14–21	8
	100

cities (one-fifth of the total), three or four groups are so designated. The general pattern thus appears to be neither one of concentration nor one of fragmentation. In the "typical" city, a modest number of organizations is named by one or more councilmen (see Table 3–3—the mean is seven groups), and a few of these groups are also perceived as influential by a majority of councilmen.

What makes a group "influential"? To avoid biasing responses, no definition of influence was provided in the interview. A wide variety of reasons for influence emerged in answer to the direct question: "What would you say makes these groups so influential —what are the main reasons for their influence?" Responses were then classified under three broad headings: objective strength (size of the group, voting power, interlocking membership with council or members of councilmen's families); perceived stake in the community (belief that the group represents an important and legitimate interest in the community); and "respect characteristics" (honesty, intelligence, activity, interest).

One-third of the councilmen who answered the question[3] confined their description to respect characteristics. An additional one-sixth answered solely in terms of either objective strength or stake in the community. The remainder—just over one-half of the respondents—gave reasons that included two or more of these components of influence. Table 3–4 presents the information, by total responses, in a somewhat more detailed form. It can be seen that group interest in council affairs, issue expertise, and the general appearance of fostering the interest of the community counts for more, as far as councilmen are concerned, than does size or voting power.[4] At the same time, spokesmen for the business community seem to fare considerably better than do those representing other interests. Only a handful of responses (included among the 136 mentioning representation of important

---

[3] This question was asked only of those who named influential groups.

[4] Zeigler implies, at several points, that legitimacy and power may in fact be indistinguishable from the viewpoint of the legislator. See Harmon Zeigler, *Interest Groups in American Society* (Englewood Cliffs, N.J.: Prentice-Hall, 1964), pp. 24–25, 274, 276.

Table 3–4
Reasons for Group Influence

Component of Influence	Times Mentioned	Total Responses*
Objective Strength:		
Size	50	
Voting power; activity or expenditures on elections	42	
Councilmen or family are group members	31	
Group is vocal; it can mobilize large number at council meetings	28	
Other (allied with bloc of council, high social status, membership overlaps with other organizations)	29	
	169	19%
Stake in Community:		
Represents business community	114	
Represents important people other than business (old residents, property owners, wealth, labor, a "cross-section" of citizens)	136	
	250	30
Respect Characteristics:		
Active and interested; attend council meetings	131	
Have council and community interests at heart	92	
Issue expertise	74	
Organizational characteristics: good leadership, high cohesion, etc.	35	
Concerned with important problems and projects	58	
Other (intelligence, competence, good sounding board, unselfish)	53	
	443	51
Total	862	100%

* Up to four responses per respondent were coded.

people other than business) alluded to labor, farmer, or vintner interests, and we have seen earlier that very few unions were included among influential groups.

It is likely that councilmen who attribute organizational influence to "activity" or "interest in council affairs" have selective perceptions—i.e., that a business-oriented councilman "sees" business approaches and requests for help, whether through the merchants association, the Chamber of Commerce, or from "those people who are important," more readily than he perceives similar but less well-organized efforts by spokesmen for labor, minorities, or conservationists. Labor or minority group activity may be perceived by councilmen as a nuisance rather than as a sign of constructive interest. A plausible alternative explanation for the juxtaposition of "activity and interest" as a major determinant of influence, and the preponderance of business organizations named, posits a difference in the efforts made by the groups themselves. It is likely that local labor unions and other nonbusiness organizations are in fact not very interested in council activities in the Bay Area communities. Robert Salisbury has argued that this is the case in many cities, and indeed we have some independent evidence on the same point for several of these communities.[5]

Up to this point, our discussion has been confined to the question of group influence. A related and equally important question might be asked about the intensity of group activity, regardless of its success. How often do groups attempt to contact councilmen? Are most group activities directed toward individual councilmen and council activities on items currently on the agenda, or do some groups spend their energies on post hoc criticism of council decisions?

Two-thirds of our respondents reported some experience with

---

[5] Robert Salisbury makes the point, in "St. Louis Politics: Relationships Among Interests, Parties and Governmental Structure," *Western Political Quarterly* 13 (1960): 498–507, that a great many union locals are simply not concerned with local politics and spend very little time with local officials. We have similar evidence from our own study of local interest group leaders in 12 of these Bay Area cities: many union officials in fact refused a request for an interview, saying that they are not active in local community affairs.

group requests for support. There were only three cities, all relatively small communities some distance from San Francisco, where all councilmen agreed that no such group approaches were made. In the remaining 79 cities, at least one councilman in each community reported some interaction with local groups. But what of the 113 councilmen (outside of the three cities where all agreed on the lack of group approaches) who could recall *no* group requests for help? Why do members of the same council disagree—some perceive group contacts and some remain completely unaware of them? Three reasons are apparent. First, some groups approach the council through the mayor or through formal hearings, rather than trying to work with individual incumbents besides the mayor. The mayor in such a community may report contacts while his fellow incumbents do not. Second, in some communities group contacts may be infrequent, and, given the high rate of turnover on most of these councils, some councilmen may not as yet have had encounters with group spokesmen. Finally, if some councilmen are openly unenthusiastic or unfriendly to local groups, requests for help are likely to be channeled through other members of the council. This is probably the case with most of the councilmen reporting no approaches, a point to which we shall return.

What methods do organization leaders employ in soliciting help? If local legislative systems were simply smaller versions of the U.S. Congress, we would expect a relatively formal interaction between group spokesmen and councilmen. We see from Table 3–5 that this is not the case. Most local groups simply pick up the telephone or visit the councilmen; a fair number of group leaders are fortunate enough to "run into" councilmen on the train, at the club, or at work; and a few councilmen are active members of the organizations in question. Formal approaches through letters, petitions, or appearances at council meetings are also reported, but not with great frequency. The local "group struggle"—if indeed it is a struggle—appears to be relatively intimate.[6]

---

[6] It is difficult to know at what exact point to set a size threshold in distinguishing between an intimate suburb (our cities include a few with a

Table 3–5
Methods Used by Local Groups
in Seeking Support from Councilmen

Type of Approach	Times Mentioned	Total Responses*
Informal Approaches:		
Social contacts, through club, work, neighborhood, commuting	24	
Councilman or family member is member of the group	15	
Luncheon or dinner (councilman and leader)	20	
Councilman is contacted by a mutual friend	6	
	65	17%
Moderate Formality:		
Phone call or visit from leader to councilman	195	
Councilman is invited to social affair or group function	20	
	215	57
Formal Approach:		
Letter or petition from group	62	
Statement or testimony at council meeting	28	
Approach through City Manager or staff	4	
	94	25
All Other	5	1
Total	379	100%

* The question: "Do any of the community groups or organizations ever contact you personally to seek your support? When these groups contact you, how do they go about doing it?" One to three responses each were coded for the 259 councilmen who answered the first part of the question in the affirmative.

population under 1,000), a small city, and a large city. (San Jose, Oakland, and Richmond are certainly not intimate suburbs.) In addition to the intimacy implied by a small population, there is also the fact that the majority of legislators work, live, and operate in the same city as the groups and individuals they affect. This is of course not the case for most state and national legislators.

Table 3–6 presents the responses to the question: "Are there any groups here in (city) which are consistently critical of what the council is doing? What groups or organizations seem to be critical?" Two major tendencies can be observed. First, relatively little criticism is perceived by councilmen (almost two-thirds of the councilmen gave a negative reply; few of the remainder named more than one organization). Second, most criticism is seen as coming from homeowners, taxpayers, or general protest groups, rather than from business interests, civic organizations, or even from "conservative" or "liberal" elements in the community. Criticism, in short, does not seem to hinge as much on either ideology or major economic issues as it does on specific day-to-day problems like zoning or traffic arrangements.

The fragmentary information provided by the 59 respondents who attempted to explain criticism indicates that ideological disagreement accounted for, at most, about one-third of the dissent. They attributed the remainder to impatience over pending community problems, dissatisfaction with past council decisions, or a desire for publicity on the part of the group or its leaders.

Tables 3–1 through 3–6 indicate that the perceived intensity of group life in the communities of the San Francisco Bay Area is low. Despite the fact that group access to councilmen is relatively easy and informal, very few groups are found to carry much influence. The average councilman names two or three "influential" groups. Less than one-quarter of these organizations represent "special interests"; about one-third are civic groups like service clubs, the PTA, and the League of Women Voters. The two groups named most frequently are the Chamber of Commerce and local neighborhood associations.

Similarly, about half of the answers to a question about the bases for influence focus on what we have called "respect characteristics" (intelligence, honesty, interest) rather than on a group's ability to mobilize support or upon the group's perceived stake in the community.

Even fewer business or labor organizations are mentioned as "consistently critical." The high incidence of homeowners and

Table 3–6
Perception of Groups "Consistently Critical" of What the Council Is Doing

Whether Critical Groups Are Perceived	Percentage of Rs (N = 407)
One or more groups named	34
No groups named	66

Type of Critical Group Named:	Percentage of 159 Groups Named
Homeowners group	20
Taxpayers association	17
General protest groups and "malcontents"	11
Chamber of Commerce	7
Merchants associations	6
"Right wing"	5
Categories of residents: business, new residents, etc.	7
All other (the only groups named by more than 5 respondents were civil rights groups, builders, and "liberals")	27
	100

taxpayers associations, together with the distribution of influential groups, leads us to infer that individuals in local communities are more active, at least in an organizational context, as homeowners than they are as businessmen or spokesmen for special interests. This interpretation raises a question: Is this picture of group life a reflection of:

1. a relatively low level of activity vis-à-vis the council by such groups as unions, civil rights organizations, and merchants associations, or
2. a moderately high level of activity by such groups even though indifference or resistance on the part of many councilmen means their efforts are not seen?

Attitudes, Orientations, and Behavior Toward Community Groups

We may assume some relation between councilmen's perceptions of community groups and the way in which they treat group spokesmen. The 69 councilmen who perceive no influential groups in their communities, for example, are considerably less likely to seek group help than are those respondents who named several groups. At the same time, there is no a priori justification for assuming that perception of influence invariably implies a favorable attitude toward local interests. A councilman who deplores the existence of "selfish interests" and resists the efforts of organized groups in trying to influence council decisions may be far more aware of such groups than the neutral or favorably inclined councilman. The relationship between perception and affect toward groups, then, is an empirical question.

We asked several questions about councilmen's general attitudes toward local groups. Are such organizations rated as important sources of information on community affairs? Are business or labor leaders relied on as heavily for advice or issue expertise as fellow councilmen, the city staff, or the press? What kind of activity weakens a group's effectiveness?

For present purposes, three questions are of considerable importance:

1. Do councilmen believe that accessibility to spokesmen for local groups is required in the performance of their roles as community decision-makers?
2. Are group activities valued or deplored?
3. Are group spokesmen co-opted as partners in the local legislative process—is their support or advice actively solicited by councilmen?

When asked: "Do you feel that, in general, you should make it easy for them [local groups] to contact you, or should you try to avoid them?" a majority of councilmen reported that they should be accessible to local groups. (See Table 3–7.) The orientations of the small minority of councilmen who believe that they should

Table 3–7
Councilmen's Responses to the Question:
"Should You Make It Easy for [Groups]
to Contact You?"

Response	Respondents (N = 433)
Make it easy	56%
Make it easy, reservations expressed	39
Avoid contacts	4
Don't know	1

avoid group contacts are probably unambiguous. The large majority who believe that they should make it easy for groups to reach them includes both those who believe that community problems are best solved through a clash of ideas and those who feel that group spokesmen are a necessary evil with a vague right to a hearing.

Responses to a second question concerning general feelings about group approaches were thus needed to separate the reluctantly accessible councilmen from those eager to deal with groups. Respondents were classified in terms of three attitudes: those who esteem, those who are neutral to, and those who reject groups. Those who esteem groups answered in terms of group utility in providing information, in mobilizing community support, or in serving as advocates for differing points of view:

> I think they should be given every opportunity to contact me. I feel that more, and not less, participation is essential, and that groups are as important, possibly more important, as individuals. When groups have decided on a position one can assume that the membership of the group has participated and thus a substantial number of people have the same position on the issue. I feel this is valuable. We have to get people to agree.

> From my legal training, I welcome any disagreement. It's the only way that the truth really comes out—the truth will emerge from intelligent opposition.

> I appreciate their doing it. I feel that it is a benefit and a necessity to know how groups feel. The more information you have before making a decision, the better off you are.

A second attitude was more neutral. A councilman with this view makes himself available to groups as part of his job or because groups have an abstract "right to a hearing." The distinction is between councilmen who see groups and/or competition between groups as potentially useful to the council or to the community, and councilmen who listen simply because it is expected of them. Examples of this second view are:

> Sure, they can come and present their views. I listen as long as they are arguing for what's best for the city.
>
> I think one should hear all sides; everyone has a right to speak his piece. I may not agree with them, but I wouldn't avoid them.
>
> Groups have a right, that's why a councilman is in business. But a councilman has a right to tell them how he feels too.

Finally, a small group of councilmen indicated their opposition to group activity and rejected the idea that value inheres in considering group claims. Most of these respondents said that they "avoid" groups whenever possible:

> I don't trust points of view formed by small groups without open hearings and the other side being represented. I must be a little bit special in this.
>
> I take a good second look. Sometimes they want things that aren't based on the good of the town. They have only a limited program.
>
> I don't think groups should contact councilmen. They should take their problems directly to the city—to the staff or to the council as a whole.

Respondents were divided as indicated in Table 3–8.

The third major question was: "Before a council decision is made, do you ever actively seek support from any of the groups you have mentioned?" Two-thirds of the city councilmen answered no to this question. These responses are particularly interesting, if relations between legislators and interest groups are conceived of as a two-way process, or a quasi-alliance system. It appears that while eight out of ten councilmen perceive influential groups and a majority believe that councilmen should be accessible to groups,

Table 3–8
Respondents' Attitudes Toward Groups

"How do you feel about the efforts of groups to make their views known to you and seek your support?"	Respondents (N = 420)
Groups are esteemed, are perceived as useful	40%
Groups are described in neutral terms; they have "a right to be heard"	40
Groups are resisted or disliked	8
Don't know, won't say	12

only a third of the councilmen ask groups for help. When it is recalled that less than a majority value groups (Table 3–8), it is evident that the "group struggle," at least in the Bay Area, takes place largely on a one-way street where relatively little traffic is seen or encouraged by those who dwell at the upper end.

Before any interpretation of these findings or their implications for local political systems can be undertaken, we must move beyond the descriptive level. We shall attempt to explain some of the differences in councilmen's perceptions and attitudes toward groups. The relationship between two sets of factors must now be considered:

1. The relation between attitudes, perceptions, and behavior of councilmen toward groups;
2. The relation between group-related variables and
   a. attitudes, perceptions, and behavior of councilmen toward other sectors in the political system;
   b. antecedent variables—background of councilmen, the city context, group affiliations, and the like.

Relation Between Respondents' Perceptions and Attitudes Toward Groups

The attempt to analyze either perceptions or attitudes of councilmen toward local groups is burdened by the complexity of separating the two variables. The problem arises from the phrasing of the major perceptual question, in which respondents were asked to name "influential" groups. The word "influential" apparently evoked an emotional response from some councilmen. A councilman who dislikes several prominent groups in his community may, especially if he is defensive about his own views, deny that "influential" groups exist. Yet the group universe may be salient to him, and he may be keenly aware that some groups are highly regarded by several of his fellow councilmen. What he is saying means, in effect: "They can't influence *me*." This answer will not tell the observer how many groups the councilman perceives, how aware he is of their activities, and precisely how he relates to them. The problem is evident in the following responses:

> *Nobody* [is influential]. There are a couple here that are suspect from the start . . . interests that are of necessity working for their own gains and ends. Their arguments shouldn't be considered as having weight unless they are valid for the city as a whole. I don't give a damn about any organization as such, especially if it has an ax to grind.

> I don't believe that there are any gradations between individuals and groups, or between groups and groups. If a man has a just cause, his influence is equal. At least it should be this way—maybe subconsciously there is influence.

In contrast, some respondents' dislike may lead them to a heightened and admitted awareness of groups. They may name three or four groups with whom their colleagues are on close terms, despite the fact that such groups carry little weight in their own thinking.

A similar problem arises with regard to those who value group activity. We would expect favorable attitudes and high salience to go together; yet some councilmen who are favorably disposed toward groups may say regretfully that there are "no influential groups here," reserving the word influential for a more central role in policy formation than the groups he admires have been able to gain. It is extremely difficult, therefore, to separate perception and cognition from affect, and it is even more troublesome to interpret the relation between components in such responses or to postulate stable relations between them.

In short, while perception of an external object should logically be assumed to be antecedent to affect, affect may cause perceptual distortion.[7] Considerable caution must be exercised in drawing inferences about the salience of community groups from responses to the question cited; any effort to establish causal relations between perception and affect is beyond the scope of this study. For present purposes we consider perception and attitude as interdependent.

We should, nonetheless, anticipate certain patterns. It would seem reasonable to expect high perception to be associated with high positive affect, and moderate or low perception to be associated with low affect, whether negative or positive. We should expect high negative affect (rejection of groups) to be associated with either of the two extremes of perception, although probably most frequently with the low, following the above reasoning.

Table 3–9 presents the necessary information in two different forms, for convenience of interpretation. It can be seen that these expectations are confirmed. We note, in Table 3–9 (b) that the majority of high perceivers are favorably disposed toward groups and that the reverse is true of low perceivers. Looking at Table 3–9 (a) and making the assumption that perception follows from attitude, we find the same sort of relationship: those who esteem groups name more influential groups than do those who are neutral or hostile toward groups.

Attitudes Toward Groups and Group Activity

We have reasoned that councilmen's attitudes toward groups depend in large part on their general conception of the political process, and we have demonstrated a consistent relationship

---

[7] The problem posed here must be distinguished from the general methodological problems arising from the use of perceptual data. In the latter case, the limitations placed on the analysis are those arising from possible differences between "reality" as perceived by the actor and "reality" as viewed from alternative vantage points. As long as we are clear on which reality we are discussing, and are sure that it is appropriate to the research question, there should be no logical or analytical difficulty.

The present problem, however, is that of separating cognitive and affective components from responses to the same question. This probably cannot be entirely solved within the framework of the research design used.

Table 3–9 (a)
Number of Influential Groups Perceived in Relation to Attitudes Toward Groups

Number of Groups Perceived	Respondent's Attitude: Esteems (N=168)	Neutral (N=179)	Rejects (N=36)
0–1	21%	31%	44%
2–3	36	38	28
4 or more	43	31	28
	100%	100%	100%

Table 3–9 (b)
Attitudes Toward Groups in Relation to Number of Influential Groups Perceived

Attitude	Number of Groups Perceived: 0–1 (N=108)	2–3 (N=138)	4 or more (N=137)
Esteems	33%	44%	53%
Neutral	52	49	40
Rejects	15	7	7
	100%	100%	100%

between acceptance or rejection of local groups and the number of groups perceived as influential. We anticipate yet another set of differences between esteemers, neutrals, and rejectors; one closely linked to councilmen's attitudes toward the group struggle. Esteemers should, in general, be more aware of "special interests" and of economic organizations. A merchants association or a realtors group is far more likely to pursue specific (and self-serving) economic goals, and to bargain, to threaten, or to "trade off" influence in pursuit of these goals, than is a service club or the League of Women Voters. Groups like the Chamber of Commerce and the homeowners organizations (which we have called "general economic interests") probably fall into an intermediate position on the political bargaining continuum. Councilmen who value groups for their contribution to the clash of ideas are also more likely than others to attribute group influence to objective strength than are those who conceive of local politics in more consensual or administrative terms.

It follows that those who are neutral in attitude are likely, when asked for a list of influential groups, to name general civic organizations and to emphasize what have been termed "respect characteristics." It is again difficult to predict the pattern of response among those who reject local groups. A perceptive rejector may respond in a way which resembles the esteemer, although he dislikes the very groups (and group tactics) which he recognizes as influential for other councilmen. Other rejectors may bring their affect and cognitions into harmony by failing to see (or at least avoiding mention of) special interests or group bargaining tactics.[8]

Table 3–10 confirms our expectations with regard to esteemers and neutrals, and indicates that the perception of influence by rejectors is highly consistent with their attitudes. A strong trend exists in regard to special interests and general economic organizations; for example, almost half of the esteemers, in contrast to less than a third of the neutrals and rejectors, include special economic interests on their list of influential organizations.

The two exceptions to this trend are the Chamber of Commerce and the general civic organizations. Almost every rejector, in contrast to roughly three-quarters of the others, names both types of groups. "Influence," for the rejector, is clearly associated strongly with those who ostensibly speak for general interests. It is likely that such groups represent less of a threat to a hostile councilman, or a less disruptive element in the local decision-making process, than do those whose demands are overtly or narrowly economic. And clearly, if this interpretation is correct, the Chamber of Commerce is seen as something other than a selfish spokesman for

---

[8] For a detailed discussion and experimental report on the near-universal human effort to bring contradictory affective and cognitive elements into balance, by misperception, compartmentalization, and other mechanisms, see Festinger, *Cognitive Dissonance.*

Table 3–10
Types of Groups Perceived in Relation to Attitudes Toward Groups (by Percentage of Respondents Mentioning Each Type)*

Types of Groups Mentioned	*Attitude Toward Groups* Esteems (N=148)	Neutral (N=140)	Rejects (N=28)
Special Interests:			
Economic organizations (merchants, realtors, unions, builders, farm groups)	47%	30%	28%
Other (civil rights groups, conservationists, veterans, senior citizens, etc.)	25	19	11
General Economic Groups:			
Homeowners, taxpayers associations	57	45	39
Chamber of Commerce, Jaycees	76	77	100
General Civic Organizations:			
Service clubs, women's groups	69	68	95

* Number of respondents = 316; total does not include those who named no influential groups. Percentages in vertical columns total more than 100% because of multiple responses; up to four responses per respondent were coded.

the business community. Indeed, it presents itself as representing the "public interest" in these communities.[9]

Table 3–11 shows the relationship between attitudes toward groups and perceived bases of group influence. We note first that those who esteem groups are markedly more cognizant of characteristics such as size and voting power—i.e., group ability to invoke sanctions—than are other councilmen. Second, it can be seen that rejectors are markedly less likely than others to attribute

[9] There is considerable evidence, from the interview protocols, that many city councilmen view the Chamber of Commerce as a disinterested service-oriented group which operates almost as a public relations arm of the council itself. A large number of respondents from different cities mentioned Chamber campaigns to attract new industry, or Chamber surveys of citizen opinion, as a major reason for Chamber influence. Councilmen said, for example, "They work for us," or "We work closely together for the city," and then went on to describe activities of the type mentioned.

influence to respect characteristics. They are the only category of councilmen that constitutes less than a majority in mentioning such characteristics. They also place almost as much emphasis on stake in society as do the esteemers.

Table 3–11
Perceived Bases of Group Influence
in Relation to Attitudes Toward Groups

	*Attitude Toward Groups**		
Perceived Bases of Influence	Esteems (N=148)	Neutral (N=144)	Rejects (N=33)
Mentions objective strength	38%	25%	23%
Mentions stake in community	47	40	46
Mentions respect characteristics	68	69	43

* Percentages in vertical columns total more than 100% because of multiple responses. Percentages are based on number of respondents (N = 325) who named at least one influential group and who also gave reasons for influence.

It appears here that strong feelings toward groups, whether negative or positive, are associated with the degree of sophistication about the group struggle. Councilmen who like or dislike groups are more conscious than those who are neutral of the impact of council decisions on community groups as well as the ability of these organizations to swing some weight in elections or in the formation of community opinion. The neutrals probably view organizations from the same perspective with which they see individuals: in terms of intelligence, interest, and perhaps generally shared values.

If the reasoning followed to this point is correct, a clear pattern of differing attitudes and perceptions is emerging. The pattern can be summarized as follows:

1. Councilmen who esteem groups also tend to perceive many influential groups and to place more emphasis on economic and special interests than do councilmen with other attitudes toward groups. They are more likely than others to attribute influence to size, voting power, money, and similar characteristics which enable groups to invoke sanctions. Their conception of the political system apparently differs sharply from others: they welcome active group participation in the political process as well as the pre-

sentation of economic claims, and they are highly cognizant of organizational activity on local political issues.

2. Councilmen who are neutral toward groups tend to perceive fewer influential groups, relatively more general civic groups, and to emphasize different components of group influence (namely, respect characteristics). Their conception of the local political process is probably close to that described by Robert Wood, Scott Greer, and others as typical of suburbia: the city council is seen as a board of directors of a corporation, searching for a "general will" of the corporation (community) rather than balancing competing interests.[10]

3. Councilmen who reject groups appear to resemble neutrals more closely than esteemers. Their level of perception is generally low, and their stated awareness of economic groups and "special interests" is even lower. In comparison with other councilmen, however, they place very little emphasis on respect characteristics, and they are also almost as aware as those who value groups of "stake in society" aspects of group influence. We have reasoned that high negative affect, like high positive affect, implies a degree of sophistication about the quality of community group life. Thus while they may view the political process in much the same way as do the neutrals, the rejectors are highly aware of, but also antagonistic to, an alternative conception of politics as interest-based.

Perception of Groups

Table 3–12 separates councilmen according to the number of groups perceived in order to examine the relationship between perception and the same variables we have considered in relation to attitudes. It will be recalled that as councilmen moved from favorable to unfavorable attitudes they placed relatively less emphasis on special interest groups and on objective strength as a basis for group influence and they were less likely to seek group support for their own proposals. We note similar differences in Table 3–12 in regard to levels of perception. Councilmen who

---

[10] See Scott Greer, *The Emerging City* (New York: The Free Press, 1962), and Robert C. Wood, *Suburbia: Its People and Their Politics* (Boston: Houghton Mifflin Co., 1959). A more detailed discussion of this body of literature is in Appendix B, pp. 170 ff.

name four or more influential groups are more likely than others to seek group support; councilmen who name many groups are more cognizant of all three bases for group influence than are others. Those who are perceptive about groups are probably more sensitive to several components of influence because they come into frequent contact with a variety of organizations that in fact differ in the sources of their strength. Breadth of perception begets contacts, which in turn increase "group sophistication." As contacts broaden, perception and sophistication probably deepen as well. This relationship, of course, hinges on the existence of a fairly broad group universe, and it is possible that in an isolated residential town the "universe" is too circumscribed to support sophisticated notions of organizational life. We shall examine this question at a later point when we consider the effect of city characteristics on councilmen's attitudes, perceptions, and orientations.

There is no question that "high" perceivers (those who name four or more influential groups) also perceive a greater variety of influential groups than do "low" perceivers. When the data given at the beginning of Table 3–12—relation between number of groups perceived and type of groups perceived—are analyzed according to the percentage of *respondents* naming a given category, a greater proportion of the "high" perceivers names *every* category.

The more interesting question is the *relative* importance of different types of organizations for councilmen with different levels of perception. It can be seen from the table that while the trends are weak, some contrasts exist. Special interest groups are relatively more important to high perceivers, while general civic and economic groups are relatively more important to low perceivers. In short, if a councilman names only one group, that group is most likely to be the Chamber of Commerce or a service club; if he adds to the list, he may then move into the world of special interests. The kinds of organizations that enter his perceptual world are also likely to help broaden his conception of group life, that is, to make him more aware of differing bases of group influence.

"Group Sophistication"

A discussion of the perception of influential groups has led us to consider sophistication regarding the group universe. We have

Table 3–12
Relation Between Level of Perception and Responses to Two Questions

	Number of Groups Perceived		
	4 or more (N=133)	2–3 (N=129)	1 (N=57)
*Types of Groups Perceived:**			
Special interest	24%	17%	9%
General economic	17	18	21
General civic	45	54	58
All other	13	12	13
Perceived Bases of Group Influence:†			
Mentions objective strength	40%	39%	15%
Mentions stake in community	59	49	43
Mentions respect characteristics	84	78	61

* Percentage of total responses. Totals for each category are: among those who name 4 or more, 525 groups; naming 2–3, 323 groups; naming 1 group, 57 groups.

† Percentage of *respondents* mentioning category. Thus percentages in vertical columns total more than 100%.

inferred from the data that those for whom groups are salient will probably have extensive exposure to group activities. In addition, we assume that this high exposure has led to some understanding of the underpinnings of group influence, or of the tools that groups can use in arguing their case. To round out our examination of possible components of "group sophistication," we must consider one further variable. This is perception of the bases of group influence, previously viewed only as a dependent variable. Those who see group influence as resting on objective strength and, to a lesser degree, on a stake in the community would more likely be aware of group efforts at exercising influence and of groups' strategies. What is attempted is a distinction between those who see community group life as something approaching an interest-based struggle and those who see groups as aggregates of disinterested individuals having no unique contribution to make as a part of a political system. Just as those who *esteem* groups differ predictably from those who do not, those for whom groups and the concept of a group struggle is salient (or who show what we have called "group sophistication") will differ predictably from those for whom it is not salient.

Two major problems arise in analyzing this relationship. First, because 170 councilmen gave multiple responses, there is considerable overlap among the three categories of respondents. This overlap will weaken any trend we find. The second difficulty is conceptual. We are not sure that "stake in the community" responses invariably signal a councilman's acceptance of interest-based politics. To say that a business or residents organization is influential because the council's decisions affect the members may be simply to repeat part of the democratic ethos: a stereotypic response roughly equivalent to "groups have a right to be heard." Despite these analytical problems, we believe that the concept of group sophistication is of sufficient importance to attempt an analysis.

We find in Table 3–13 that our expectations are fulfilled, although the relations are weak. Sophisticated councilmen are more aware than others of group contacts, and more likely to seek group help; but in both cases the differences are quite small. We conclude that while the concept of "group sophistication" is probably a valuable one from an analytical standpoint, the indicator we are using is not satisfactory. Better results could be obtained from a measure that clearly dichotomized respondents; yet a problem of validity might arise in this case, since the overlap in councilmen's responses no doubt indicates a complex set of perceptions and cognitions that defies conceptual elegance.

A Typology of Role Orientations Toward Groups

It seems wise at this point to combine several of the indices already considered in order to proceed with the analysis in a more manageable form. It would be desirable to utilize direct questions about role orientations, but we have seen that the direct question concerning councilmen's own expectations about their behavior toward interest groups[11] did not prove to be sufficiently discrim-

[11] The question: "Do you feel that, in general, you should make it easy for them to contact you, or should you try to avoid them?"

Table 3–13
Relation Between Perceived Bases of Group Influence and Responses to Selected Questions

Affirmative Responses	Mentions Objective Strength (N=116)*	Mentions Stake (N=167)	Mentions Respect (N=253)
Perceives group contacts for support	78%	72%	69%
Seeks group support for own proposals	42	44	31

* Based on number of respondents mentioning each basis for group influence. Thus the number in the three rows is greater than our N of 365.

inating for our purposes. Ninety-five percent of the respondents answered, with only minor reservations, that they "should make it easy" for groups to contact them. Yet we have also seen that respondents differed in their attitudes toward groups and probably in their accessibility as well. Most respondents believe, in short, that it is part of their role to be accessible to groups, but not necessarily *eager* in their relationships. This information is of limited utility: it will not tell us which respondents believe, and act on the belief, that groups should have an *active* part in the process of policy formation for the community. Thus, we divided respondents in terms of three basic attitudes: those who esteem groups and/or "the group struggle"; those who are neutral toward groups; and those who reject groups. Building upon these attitudinal measures, we distinguished between three types of councilmen—Pluralists, Antagonists, and Tolerants.

The procedure followed in constructing these types is outlined in detail in Appendix C. Our primary aim was to supplement attitudinal indicators with measures of difference in the salience of the group universe. There is no entirely satisfactory indicator for salience, since ability to name groups in response to an interview question does not in itself provide information about the significance of groups to the respondent in comparison with other community actors. Nor does the number of influential groups named tell much about the respondent's ability to differentiate among these organizations. Two indicators were therefore employed: one tapping a dimension we can term "extent of perception," the other tapping a related dimension, "group sophistication."

For the first dimension, the best measure is number of groups named in response to the question about "influential" groups. For the second dimension, "group sophistication" or sensitivity to groups as claims-presenters, responses to the question "Why are these groups so influential?" were used. The measure is not ideal. We lack, however, a direct question asking for opinions on the place of groups in the political process. We assume that the combination of number of groups perceived and perceived bases for group influence will provide a rough measure of salience.

The 412 respondents who could be classified in these terms were distributed as follows:

	Perceives Many Groups	
*Attitude Toward Groups:**	*Sophisticated*	*Unsophisticated*
Esteems	100 Pluralists	34 Tolerants
Neutral	71 Tolerants	45 Tolerants
Rejects	15 Antagonists	8 Antagonists
	Perceives Few Groups	
	Sophisticated	*Unsophisticated*
Esteems	12 Tolerants	24 Tolerants
Neutral	10 Tolerants	51 Tolerants
Rejects	7 Antagonists	4 Tolerants

* An additional 31 respondents gave no answer to the question on attitudes. All 31 perceived few groups; three would be classed as "sophisticated" on the basis of reasons for group influence of the one group they named, while the remaining 28 are "unsophisticated." All 31 were classed as Tolerants. Thus we analyze a total of 282 Tolerant responses in the study.

We anticipate a number of contrasts between the three types of councilmen. We expect Pluralists to perceive more economic groups and spokesmen for "special interests" than Tolerants or

Antagonists. They should be more aware of group requests for support, and more important, their own behavior should differ in that they should be more likely than others to seek group support for their own proposals. Finally, they should place more value on groups as information sources than do others.[12]

No statement can be made with any degree of confidence about the causal direction of these behavioral and evaluative factors. If group support is sought, it may be in part because groups are considered expert; on the other hand, continued reliance on group support may in itself *engender* an expectation of group expertise on community problems. Because we expect a greater sensitivity to community opinion on the part of respondents who conceive of politics as a process of balancing competing interests, we expect Pluralists to be both more dependent on and more aware of a variety of extra-council structures.

Our expectations with regard to Tolerants and Antagonists are implicit in the foregoing: Tolerants and Antagonists should be less receptive to groups and group leaders as information sources, less likely to perceive group contacts, and less likely to seek group support for their own proposals.

It is difficult to predict differences between the Tolerants and Antagonists. Behaviorally, the Tolerants should lie at a point between Antagonists and Pluralists. For example, they should be more likely to seek group support than are the Antagonists, but less likely than the Pluralists. At the same time, these two sets of councilmen may be indistinguishable for all practical purposes as far as perceptual and even some attitudinal measures are concerned, because, to repeat a point made earlier, low cognition and negative affect may be functionally equivalent: what is disliked is eventually, where possible, ignored. It is possible, looking at respondents from the point of view of the organizations involved,

---

12 It should be recalled that questions concerning perceived group contacts, the value of groups as information sources, councilmen's own efforts to seek group help, and the like are entirely separate from those used in building the initial typology of role orientations. It is perfectly possible, for example, for a councilman to name no "influential" groups and yet to have experienced (and to recall at the present time) group requests for help.

that fewer approaches are made to avowed Antagonists than to Tolerants, especially if group resources for making such approaches are limited. In this case we would expect Antagonists to perceive fewer group contacts than do Tolerants because, in fact, fewer contacts are made. But this calls for the assumption that responses to interview questions were made without affective distortions. It also assumes a high group awareness of respondents' attitudes. In light of both the unwillingness of respondents to put themselves on record as trying to avoid group contacts, and the high turnover rate of incumbents on these councils,[13] we cannot be certain that groups know enough of individual councilmen's views to be able to modify their tactics accordingly. Thus no firm prediction can be stated on the subject of perceptual differences between Antagonists and Tolerants. Later, when we relate councilmen's group role orientations to other role sectors, some sharper distinctions between the two types can be tested.

Table 3–14 clearly indicates that Pluralists are considerably more aware of group contacts than are Tolerants and Antagonists. Almost every Pluralist, in contrast to two-thirds of the Tolerants and half of the Antagonists, reports such group efforts. With one exception, there is very little difference in the *methods* that groups use in reaching the three types of councilmen. Antagonists apparently are successful in maintaining sufficient distance from group spokesmen to avoid or prevent informal approaches, but the mixture of very formal and moderately formal techniques is about the same for all councilmen.

It is of course likely that many councilmen, including Antagonists, fail to recognize or interpret some informal group contacts as such. A chance discussion of an impending zoning change with a golfing partner may be, from the point of view of the partner, an informal "sounding" on the subject—assuming that the partner is a member of a concerned homeowners or business group. Such a discussion may be perceived as a "contact" by a councilman who is open to group approaches. If, however, the conversation is not seen by the councilman-golfer as a "contact," it is not, strictly

[13] Mean years of service for all respondents was 4.7 years.

Table 3–14
Relation Between Councilmen's Interest Group Role Orientations and Perception of Group Contacts

	Interest Group Role Orientation		
	Pluralist (N=100)	Tolerant (N=257)	Antagonist (N=30)
Contacts Are Perceived (directed to individual councilman or to council as a whole)	93%	66%	50%
	*Percentage of Total Responses**		
Method of Contact	(N=91)	(N=153)	(N=13)
Informal (social or work contact; respondent or fellow-councilman is a member of group)	12%	11%	0%
Moderately formal (phone call or visit; invitation to group function; contact through intermediary)	66	63	78
Formal (appearance at hearing; letter or petition; group statement to press; contact through staff or City Manager)	22	26	22
	100%	100%	100%

* Based on responses of those councilmen who perceive group contacts. Many of those who perceived contacts, however, did not elaborate on the methods used by groups.

speaking, a part of the perceptual and behavioral world with which we are now concerned.[14]

[14] There is some evidence from the author's interviews with 49 group leaders in 12 of these cities that more group leader/councilman interaction takes place

Table 3–15 presents a breakdown of influential groups named by the three categories of councilmen. It will be recalled that we anticipate a Pluralist emphasis on special interests and economic organizations. We expect the Antagonists to be more cognizant of special interests than are the Tolerants because of their greater "group sophistication." Two rather striking trends emerge from

Table 3–15
Relation Between Interest Group Role Orientation
and Types of Groups Named as Influential
(by Percentage of Respondents)*

	Interest Group Role Orientation		
Types of Groups Named as Influential	Pluralist (N=100)	Tolerant (N=217)	Antagonist (N=27)
Special Interests:			
Economic organizations (merchants, realtors, builders, unions, farm organizations)	49%	26%	40%
Other (civil rights groups, conservationists, veterans, senior citizens)	29	14	10
General Economic Groups:			
Homeowners and taxpayers	73	30	40
Chamber of Commerce, Jaycees	77	54	90
General Civic Organizations:			
Service clubs	44	22	23
Women's organizations (LWV, PTA, AAUW, etc.)	31	23	13

* Vertical columns total more than 100% because up to four groups were coded for each respondent.

---

than was indicated in response to interview questions. Many councilmen, for example, who are claimed as "active" members by the organization leaders do not themselves mention their group affiliation in our interviews. We assume that these affiliations are simply not as important (or salient) to the councilmen as they are to the group leaders. Thus while there is probably a considerable amount of politically relevant conversation that does not appear in our data, its low salience to the councilman leads us to discount its importance.

the table. First, the Pluralists are more aware of all but one category of local groups (the Chamber of Commerce and Jaycees) than are their fellow councilmen. Second, general economic groups (the Chamber of Commerce and homeowners associations) are by far the most important organizations for all councilmen. Apparently, these two kinds of groups, which purport to speak for the interests of the business and property-owning community, press claims or pursue goals that cannot be ignored. This point is particularly striking with regard to the Chamber of Commerce, which a majority of every category of councilman, including the relatively unaware and neutral Tolerants as well as an overwhelming majority of both Pluralists and Antagonists, perceives as influential.

We may also note that our expectations with regard to special interests are fulfilled. Pluralists are more likely than Tolerants to see special economic interests as influential, with Antagonists falling into an intermediate position. Pluralists are markedly more aware of civil rights groups, conservationists, and other noneconomic special interests than are either Tolerants or Antagonists.[15] This relatively high awareness is consistent with their view of groups as an integral part of the political bargaining process.

At the same time, Pluralists place considerable emphasis on the Chamber of Commerce, homeowners groups, and service clubs. We conclude that these three types of organizations are of major importance in representing key interests of residents of Bay Area communities (sometimes because they include among their members men whose voices cannot be ignored by local policy-makers).

Our information thus far has been limited to councilmen's perceptions of groups. One question concerning role behavior is of particular interest in validating our assumption that there is a systematic connection between councilmen's role orientations and

---

15 Many demands made on city councils by civil rights groups and spokesmen for senior citizens are, of course, economic. It should be recalled, however, that our data were collected in 1966 and 1967, before civil rights organizations had shifted from a focus on integration to demands for loans to ghetto business and the like. We would argue that the demands of these groups, while geared indirectly to the economic betterment of Blacks and other minority groups were, prior to 1968, largely confined to symbolic or long-range improvements. Thus we do not classify such organizations with more unambiguously economic groups such as merchants, realtors, and unions.

their concrete behavior: Do councilmen seek group support before a council decision is made? We expect the Pluralists to be most active in seeking group help and the Antagonists to be least interested in such assistance. Those who value local group activity can reasonably be expected to make allies of local groups; those who are antagonistic would be quite inconsistent to do so unless they were acting in self-defense on a council where the majority used such alliances successfully. And the Tolerants (largely unaware of, or indifferent to, the group universe) should probably fall into an intermediate position. Table 3–16 presents the data. The perceptions and attitudes of councilmen concerning community groups are indeed reflected in their concrete behavior. A clear majority of Pluralists, in contrast to only 10 percent of the Antagonists and about one-quarter of the Tolerants, seek group support on issues before the council.

The remainder of the table presents no sharp contrasts between the three groups of councilmen, but the data are included for the information they provide on the role that groups play in supporting councilmen. The most important group support function is apparently an active one, namely, helping the councilman make his case or sell his ideas to both the public and his fellow councilmen. This is a far cry from the group's "right to be heard," so often cited by Tolerants as their reason for making themselves available to group spokesmen. It is suprising that even half of those Tolerants (or about 15 percent of all Tolerants) rely on groups in this fashion. Next in importance are two functions which David Truman stresses in regard to national groups: the provision of information on public attitudes and on the issue itself.[16] Here it is interesting to note that issue expertise is of considerably less importance than information "on the public pulse." (The final function—the councilman's effort to convince the group—is not, strictly speaking, a request for concrete support, unless we assume

---

[16] ". . . the legislator is constantly in need of relevant information. Access is likely to be available to groups somewhat in proportion to their ability to meet this need. . . . The knowledge required by politicians may be divided into two types: technical knowledge . . . and political knowledge of the relative strength of competing claims and of the consequences of alternative decisions on a policy issue." David Truman, *The Governmental Process*, pp. 333–334.

Table 3–16

Relation Between Interest Group Role Orientation and Seeking of Group Support*

	Interest Group Role Orientation		
	Pluralist (N=100)	Tolerant (N=252)	Antagonist (N=30)
Percentage of Councilmen Who Seek Group Support	57	27	10
Type of Groups from Whom Support Is Sought:	Percentage of Total Responses (N=196)		
Chamber of Commerce, Jaycees	21%	25%	—†
Homeowners groups, taxpayers	25	23	
Service clubs	17	8	
Merchants groups	7	8	
Women's groups	5	5	
All other, including *ad hoc* organizations (no category was mentioned by more than 4% of the respondents)	25	31	
	100%	100%	
Kinds of Support Sought:	(N=131)		
Help at hearings or in trying to sell councilman's position to others	61%	55%	—†
Information on public attitudes, on potential impact of proposal on groups	19	12	
Facts, expertise, background information	6	9	
Effort to convince group of correctness of councilman's position	14	24	
	100%	100%	

* The question: "Before a Council decision is made, do you ever actively seek support from any of the groups you have mentioned? (IF YES): What kind of support do you seek? May I ask from which groups you have sought support?"

† We have not computed percentages for the responses of the three Antagonists who seek support, since figures computed on such a small base are misleading and meaningless.

that he is building up a following to endorse his stand in a future election or referendum on the issue. He is probably simply requesting understanding or moral backing.)

It is significant that the five categories of organizations most frequently asked for help are the same five that lead the list of influential organizations. Once again, the Chamber, homeowners groups, and service clubs far outstrip other organizations—this time as working allies of councilmen. In light of the kind of support which councilmen seek from such groups, we are probably safe in our inference that these three groupings contain most of the political stratum, or the individuals and interests to be reckoned with in the communities studied.[17] This is not to say that other interest groups are unimportant, but rather to suggest that in the view of Bay Area councilmen they do not carry much weight on council decisions. And, judging from the nature of the five groups that are both "influential" and sought-after, it is the businessmen and homeowning residents who possess the skills and status to dominate the political stratum.[18]

A final question remains: Just how important are local groups, in comparison with other individuals and institutions in the same community, in providing advice and information to councilmen? A related question, of course, is the comparison of Pluralist, Tolerant, and Antagonist attitudes toward groups as information sources. Once again, we would expect Pluralists to value groups more than do others, although we assume that they, like other councilmen, will rely most heavily on the city manager, city staff, and fellow councilmen.

Table 3–17 shows councilmen's responses to a question asking

---

[17] The "political stratum" is a term borrowed from Robert Dahl, *Who Governs? Democracy and Power in an American City* (Chicago: University of Chicago Press, 1956). We have no wish to enter into the community power controversy. Thus we shall use terms like leaders, political stratum, and elites in the discussion that follows to designate those individuals who assume, or are likely to assume, either official or informal leadership roles in the community—without further implication intended.

[18] This is no news to the student of local government. See Robert Wood's discussion of this point in *Suburbia*. For a partial exception, however, see Bennett M. Berger, *Working Class Suburb: A Study of Auto Workers in Suburbia* (Berkeley: University of California Press, 1960).

them to rank potential sources of advice on issues before the council.[19] Two trends are evident. First, expert advice (from city officials and other councilmen) is clearly valued more highly than that tendered by either the general populus or spokesmen for community organizations and the press. A vast majority of councilmen, regardless of role orientation, value the city manager's opinions; in contrast, a very small proportion rank group spokesmen, the press, or people in the city as first or second in importance. Second, however, we note a distinctive and consistent contrast between Pluralists and others. Organization leaders in the city are considerably more important to the Pluralists than are "people in the city generally." For Tolerants and Antagonists, the order is reversed. Once again, the Pluralists seem more attuned to *group* advice than to offerings of unaffiliated individuals. In contrast, Tolerants and Antagonists seem to show their mistrust of the group process by their reliance on the unaffiliated or "disinterested" individual.

In summary, the following general differences have emerged between three types of councilmen. Pluralists are most likely to perceive group contacts, and they are generally aware of a wider variety of groups than are their fellow incumbents. Although Pluralists as well as others seek out city officials as their main source of advice, they are less likely than other councilmen to depend on the expertise of the city manager and city staff. Group spokesmen are more important to the Pluralists than to others, both as a source of advice on issues and as working allies on matters before the council.

Antagonists are the least aware of group contacts or requests for help. They rarely seek either group advice or contacts. This avoidance is not explained simply by a reluctance to seek outside help, for they are more receptive than others to advice from "people in

---

[19] This is one of four questions of the same general type, all of which showed similar patterns of response. One question asked councilmen to categorize eight potential information sources as "very important," "important," "not very important," or "not important at all." The contrast between Pluralists and others is striking: 84% see organization leaders as "very important" or "important," in comparison with 70% of the Tolerants and 36% of the Antagonists.

Table 3–17
Relation Between Interest Group Role Orientation and Ranking of Sources of Advice*

Sources of Advice About Council Issues	*Interest Group Role Orientation* Pluralist (N=73)	Tolerant (N=227)	Antagonist (N=22)
	(percentage of councilmen ranking source as first or second)		
Experts:			
City Manager or other city officials	70%	84%	77%
Other councilmen	60	61	59
Spokesmen:			
Organizational leaders in city	29	13	5
Influential individuals	22	15	23
Newspaper(s)	1	5	0
General Population:			
People who come to council meetings	7	8	0
People in the city generally	12	22	23
People in my neighborhood	1	2	0

* The question: "Now we would like you to tell us from whom you get the best advice about issues before the Council. Please rank the following in terms of the best advice you can get: (1) city manager and other city officials, (2) other councilmen, (3) newspaper(s), (4) organization leaders in city, (5) influential individuals in city, (6) people in the city generally, (7) people in my neighborhood, (8) people who come to council meetings."

the city" and/or "influential individuals." Interaction between group spokesmen and Antagonists is limited to relatively formal occasions—letters, petitions, telephone calls, and the like—in contrast to social and work contacts.

Tolerants are in an intermediate position. They are less likely than the Pluralists, but more likely than the Antagonists, to seek group help or advice. They are moderately aware of group contacts, and these group-to-Tolerant contacts take place on both an informal and formal basis. They are the *least* likely of all councilmen to name spokesmen for *special* economic interests as influential, and they are the *most* attuned of all councilmen to advice from the general public and the city staff. Thus, while they believe in general terms in accessibility to the public, their conception of local politics appears to be the very antithesis of an interest-based bargaining process or a "group struggle."

Chapter 4

Interest Group Role Orientations: Antecedents

Legislative behavior is subject to a variety of explanations. A representative's attitudes and mode of operation can, for example, be explained in at least two different fashions. The observer can probe the individual's economic and social origins, his early political experiences, and the manner in which he was recruited into his present office. His political career pattern, as well as his social and economic history, may provide strong clues about his present attitudes toward both his constituents and his fellow legislators and, in turn, about his role behavior as a congressman, state senator, or city councilman.[1]

A different approach consists of relating legislative behavior to the economic and institutional-legal environment within which that behavior takes place. Using this approach, legislator-constituent relations, voting patterns, and the content of legislative outputs can be explained in large part as flowing naturally from the

---

[1] For a sample of some of the work done on the relation between legislative behavior and prior socialization and recruitment experiences, see Donald R. Matthews, *U.S. Senators and Their World* (Chapel Hill: University of North Carolina Press, 1960); Wahlke et al., *The Legislative System,* Part II; James D. Barber, *The Lawmakers: Recruitment and Adaptation to Legislative Life* (New Haven: Yale University Press, 1965); Joseph Schlesinger, *Ambition and Politics: Political Careers in the United States* (Chicago: Rand-McNally, 1966); and Kenneth Prewitt, *The Recruitment of Political Leaders: A Study of Citizen-Politicians* (Indianapolis: Bobbs-Merrill, 1971).

environment in which those policies are made.[2] Those who study the relations between environmental factors and policy outcomes do not argue that the personal backgrounds or political predispositions of decision-makers are unimportant. They simply concentrate on that part of the variation in the outcomes of different legislative systems that can be explained by environmental differences and ignore for the most part the political factors that may intervene between environment and policies. Thus the "input-output" analyst may find that councilmen in a suburb inhabited largely by young middle-class parents will spend proportionally more on education and amenities than will their counterparts in an industrial or retirement community. For such an analyst, the intricacies of councilman/constituent relations may be interesting but he will not dwell on this type of information. He has found, in the past, that "political" variables are less useful for his purposes than economic indicators.[3]

Our present concern with councilman/interest group relations demands an eclectic approach. On the one hand, it is likely that individual career patterns of councilmen (e.g., the means they employed to gain public office) affect to some degree their relations with group spokesmen and other constituents and their voting preferences as councilmen. On the other hand, the economic and institutional-legal environment within which they act may effectively limit both the avenues to local office and the range of choices on the council agenda. The attitudes and behavior of councilmen, toward community groups and also in regard to the content of legislation, are likely to be a product of their present political/economic environment as well as their personal political history. The problem of establishing the antecedents of councilmen's role orientations toward groups is particularly intricate because the quality of interest group life in the councilman's city is limited in part by the political/economic environment. Thus his own orien-

---

[2] See for examples of this approach Dawson and Robinson, "Inter-Party Competition"; and Dye, *Politics, Economics and The Public*. For a survey of much of the literature in this field, see Jacob and Lipsky, "Outputs, Structure and Power."

[3] For a more detailed critique of this literature, see Chapter 7.

Figure 4–1
Environment, Group Universe, Political Careers, and Councilmen's Group Role Orientations

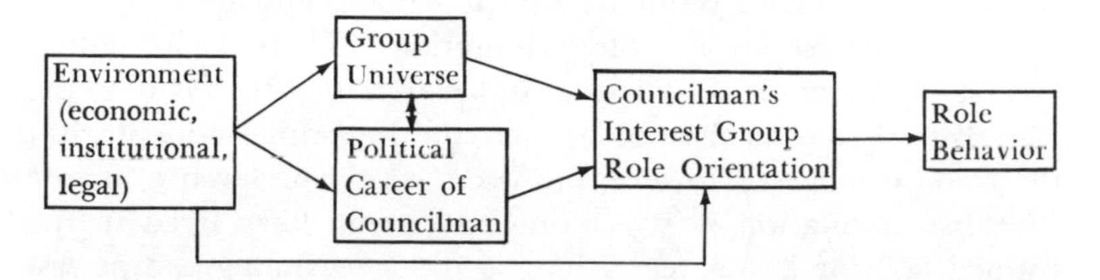

tation hinges in all likelihood on his personal political history and the local interest group universe he confronts, *both* of which are in part results of the general environment. The outline of the relationships that must be examined is shown in Figure 4–1. We deal in this chapter with the relation between individual backgrounds, career patterns, and interest group role orientations. We also examine, briefly, the tie between group role orientations and the urban environment, but we reserve our major discussion of this last subject for Chapter 7.

Personal Characteristics

We do not expect to find any sharp contrasts in the social and economic background of Pluralists, Tolerants, and Antagonists for two reasons. First, the almost universally high status of councilmen in these California cities precludes the use of socioeconomic characteristics as explanatory variables. (Over 80 percent of our respondents earn $10,000 or more per year; considerably over half are employed in managerial or professional positions.) Second, there are no powerful theoretical reasons for anticipating correlations between socioeconomic characteristics and the interest group role orientations of councilmen. We might, at first glance, expect group sophistication to be a result of education. However, this kind of explanation is probably more useful in dealing with the general population where, for example, it is well established that levels of political information and political efficacy are highly correlated with education.[4] We present data, nevertheless, in Tables 4–1 through 4–4 to check the accuracy of our expectations.

Table 4–1 indicates that there is no strong relationship between the age or length of residence of councilmen and the choice of differing interest group role orientations. There is a slightly greater tendency for *young* men and *new residents* to choose the Pluralist orientation than older men and long-time residents, but the trend is modest. However, an even greater preference for the Pluralist orientation exists among those who have lived in the council city for 20–29 years than is the case among the newest arrivals. It is tempting to attribute the modest correlation between youth and brief residence and the Pluralist orientation to an enthusiasm for politics associated with a lack of political experience. Data on the relative length of service of councilmen do not support this point: there is no significant contrast in the number of years spent in office by the three types of respondents; the small differences that do exist indicate that *Antagonists* are the least experienced incumbents.[5] We therefore view the slight difference in age and residential experience as probably not relevant to our attempt to trace antecedents of differing interest group role orientations.

We find that preference for the Pluralist orientation *increases* with formal education, while preference for the Tolerant orientation seems to be associated with relatively little schooling (Table 4–2). The link between formal schooling and the Pluralist orientation is not surprising, given the degree of group sophistication built into that role. The Tolerant role is a far easier one to take,

---

[4] See, for example, Angus Campbell et al., *The American Voter* (New York: John Wiley and Sons, 1964); Herbert McClosky, "Consensus and Ideology in American Politics," *American Political Science Review* 58 (1964): 361–379; Gabriel Almond and Sidney Verba, *The Civic Culture: Political Attitudes and Democracy in Five Nations* (Princeton: Princeton University Press, 1963); Kenneth P. Langton, *Political Socialization* (New York: Oxford University Press, 1969), especially pp. 142–160.

[5] The relationship between the length of service of city councilmen and their interest group role orientations is as follows: One-two years: Pluralists 26%, Tolerants 26%, Antagonists 40%; three-seven years: Pluralists 45%, Tolerants 50%, Antagonists 35%; eight years or more: Pluralists 29%, Tolerants 24%, Antagonists 25%.

Table 4–1
Relation Between Age and Length of Residence of Councilmen and Interest Group Role Orientation

	Age of Councilmen				
Interest Group Role Orientation	Under 40 (N=59)	41–45 (N=61)	46–50 (N=72)	51–55 (N=58)	56 or more (N=95)
Pluralist	31%	20%	23%	21%	23%
Tolerant	66	75	67	72	72
Antagonist	3	5	10	7	5
	100%	100%	100%	100%	100%
	Length of Residence in Council City				
	Under 10 years (N=66)	10–14 (N=77)	15–19 (N=48)	20–29 (N=75)	30 or more (N=80)
Pluralist	29%	18%	17%	31%	20%
Tolerant	65	73	77	61	76
Antagonist	6	9	6	8	4
	100%	100%	100%	100%	100%

since it requires less awareness and less interaction between councilmen and actors outside the council; hence it is very much preferred by the less-educated councilmen. In contrast, there is no relationship between family income and the choice of an interest group role orientation.

Table 4–3 warns us against the easy assumption that education alone predisposes men to take the Pluralist orientation, for here we see a distinct connection between relatively low-status occupations (clerical, sales, and craft jobs) and the Pluralist role. The most plausible explanation, in this case, is that men in these occupations are less likely than those in managerial positions to accept an apolitical-managerial norm for council behavior. We shall have occasion to deal with this norm in some detail in Chapter 6 in considering purposive roles; suffice it to say, at present, that this position is particularly common in wealthy suburban

Table 4–2
Relation Between Education and Family Income
of Councilmen and Interest Group Role Orientation

Interest Group Role Orientation	Less than high school graduate (N=20)	H. S. graduate but not college graduate (N=153)	College graduate or more (N=176)
	Education		
Pluralist	10%	22%	26%
Tolerant	80	73	66
Antagonist	10	5	7
	100%	100%	99%*

	Under $10,000 (N=63)	$10,000–14,999 (N=102)	$15,000–19,999 (N=68)	$20,000 or more (N=105)
	Family Income			
Pluralist	19%	24%	25%	24%
Tolerant	76	71	65	70
Antagonist	6	5	10	6
	101%*	100%	100%	100%

* Discrepancies due to rounding.

communities. It is based on the assumption that the council's major task is to seek for a general community good, *without the necessity for a clash of interests.* Those in clerical, sales, or craft occupations are considerably less likely than businessmen to share the idea of a managerial consensus over community politics. They are thus more likely than others to choose a group role orientation that posits the need for brokerage tasks, namely, that of the Pluralist.

Table 4–4 simply underlines a point made earlier about the Tolerants. There are no sharp differences between Republican and Democratic preferences for group role orientations; the only striking finding is the strong tendency for Independents to choose the Tolerant orientation. The Independent rejects the idea of strong party loyalty, and by implication, he may also ignore or

Table 4–3
Relation Between Occupational Status and Interest Group Role Orientation

	Occupational Status			
Interest Group Role Orientation	Managerial (N=146)	Professional (N=87)	Clerical, sales, and crafts (N=63)	All other* (N=41)
Pluralist	21%	23%	33%	12%
Tolerant	72	69	62	78
Antagonist	7	8	5	10
	100%	100%	100%	100%

* The majority of respondents in this category are either retired or housewives. Also included, however, are a few farm employees and unskilled workers.

oppose the interest aggregation activities that political parties can perform. In short, he may be relatively apolitical.[6] The Tolerant orientation toward local groups is the direct equivalent to the Independent stance in regard to parties, and as such, it is the natural choice for an Independent.

We indicated our belief, prior to examining the data in Tables 4–1 through 4–4, that a knowledge of socioeconomic and other personal characteristics of councilmen will not take us very far in explaining the choice of interest group role orientations. To some degree this expectation was correct: in no instance did we find that the *majority* of those with attribute X chose the Pluralist orientation, while those with non-X became Tolerants or Antagonists. At the same time, a few modest trends have appeared:

1. Young men are more likely to be Pluralists than are their older colleagues.

2. College graduates prefer the Pluralist orientation to a greater extent than high school graduates; the least-educated councilmen are most likely to become Tolerants.

---

[6] See Bernard Berelson et al., *Voting* (Chicago: University of Chicago Press, 1954), for a rather discouraging account of the political efficacy, information level, and motives of the independent voter.

Table 4–4
Relation Between Party Identification and Interest Group Role Orientation

Interest Group Role Orientation	Party Identification		
	Republican (N=175)	Democrat (N=137)	Independent (N=29)
Pluralist	27%	22%	7%
Tolerant	67	71	86
Antagonist	6	7	7
	100%	100%	100%

3. Those in relatively low-status occupations are more likely to be Pluralist than those in managerial or professional positions.

4. Independents show a stronger preference for the Tolerant orientation than do those who identify with one of the two major parties; there is no significant difference between Republican and Democratic choices of interest group role orientations.

We thus have some clues to the choice of group role orientations: young, well-educated men and/or those in low-status positions are more predisposed to become Pluralists than others, while their opposite numbers are more likely to be Tolerants. Antagonists come in about equal proportions from all walks of socioeconomic life.

Characteristics of Council Cities

The next question to be answered concerns the councilmen's environment. Such factors as city size and industrial complexity or the educational level of the citizens may be very important for several reasons: they may affect the quantity and complexity of the interest group life in these cities; they may delimit the constellation of concrete problems with which councilmen and group members must cope; and they may be associated with differing patterns of recruitment for public office.

The entire set of relations implied by the foregoing is explored in detail in Chapter 7. We want to examine here two sets of environmental factors in relation to the choice of interest group role orientations by individual councilmen: first, the *potential for conflict* over relatively scarce public resources, implicit in variations in city size and industrialization; and second, the *potential for public participation,* implicit in differences in family income and citizens' educational level. We predict that interest groups are most likely to be active in large and socially diverse cities. Similarly, we anticipate more intensive group activity in settings where citizens possess the skills (implied by high education and high socioeconomic status) to press their claims effectively. Where groups are most active, diverse, and skillful, councilmen are most likely to adopt the Pluralist orientation.

The information in Table 4–5, taken as a whole, confirms these expectations. A considerably larger proportion of Pluralists emerge in large cities and in industrial cities than in the smaller, residential communities. Similarly, the Tolerant orientation is most common in very small and nonindustrial towns and is less frequent in the large or industrial cities. Once again, Antagonists appear in roughly equal numbers in all categories of cities. As predicted, the Pluralist orientation seems most appropriate in environments where social pluralism is also likely, i.e., in the urban, industrial setting.

A clear relation also appears when we compare the educational and socioeconomic status of the residents in council cities to the frequency with which their councilmen choose the Pluralist orientation (see Table 4–6). If our previous reasoning is correct, this relationship arises because the existence of educational skills fosters an active group life in the community, which in turn makes it more acceptable or desirable for councilmen to draw group spokesmen into the policy-making process. In communities where the potential for participation is low, the Tolerant orientation is more desirable or appropriate.

Recruitment Patterns and Group Role Orientations

We have also predicted that environmental factors will affect the way in which councilmen are recruited for office and that re-

Table 4–5
Relation Between City Population, Industrialization, and Interest Group Role Orientation

Interest Group Role Orientation	*Population* Under 2,500 (N=44)	2,500–9,999 (N=110)	10,000–49,999 (N=158)	50,000 or more (N=101)
Pluralist	5%	26%	22%	36%
Tolerant	90	67	68	59
Antagonist	5	7	10	5
	100%	100%	100%	100%

	Industrialization (percentage of urbanized land in industrial or commercial use) 0–4% (N=64)	5–9% (N=66)	10–19% (N=97)	20–100% (N=96)
Pluralist	12%	24%	27%	27%
Tolerant	79	65	67	66
Antagonist	9	11	6	7
	100%	100%	100%	100%

cruitment patterns are related to group role orientations. Pluralists are more likely to emerge from an "interest-oriented" than from a "service-oriented" background; Tolerants and Antagonists probably come to the council via prior community service that is relatively divorced from controversy or claims-presentation.

The political careers of councilmen can be divided into three rough phases: general political socialization experiences (prior to those which led to the council position); direct recruitment experiences; and on-the-job experiences. In a related study dealing with the same population, it was reported that differences in general political socialization bear little relationship to the specialized roles later assumed by city councilmen.[7] Such variables as time of socialization, socialization agents, and external events associated

[7] Prewitt, *The Recruitment of Political Leaders.*

Table 4–6
Relation Between Education and Income Level of Population in Council Cities and Interest Group Role Orientation

Interest Group Role Orientation	*Percentage of Population with High School Degree*		
	49.9% or less (N=121)	50–64.9% (N=139)	65% or more (N=124)
Pluralist	18%	26%	32%
Tolerant	74	64	64
Antagonist	8	10	4
	100%	100%	100%
	Median Income of Residents		
	$6,749 or less (N=139)	$6,750–7,750 (N=120)	$7,751 or more (N=125)
Pluralist	19%	24%	33%
Tolerant	73	66	62
Antagonist	8	10	5
	100%	100%	100%

with socialization did not affect either the representational style or purposive role orientations assumed by councilmen. Although the relation between these initial socialization experiences and the interest group role orientation was not studied, we have no reason to expect predictive value in this data insofar as group roles are concerned. The data (not shown) confirmed this expectation: no consistent relation between the interest group role orientation and early socialization experiences of councilmen was found.[8]

[8] The strongest relationship to emerge was between the interest group role orientation and initial time of political socialization: 81% of the Antagonists, in contrast to 70% of the Tolerants and 68% of the Pluralists, first became aware of or interested in politics as high school students or earlier. We find no support in the literature and no logical explanation for this difference of 13%, and no support from other data on initial socialization experiences in our own study; thus we do not discuss the point in the text.

Councilmen were asked to describe their activity and involvement in community affairs before they became city councilmen. We expected their experiences during this recruitment phase to have considerable relevance to the way in which they function as councilmen. Those who first became interested in community politics through a local reform movement, a battle over incorporation, or the struggles of a neighborhood association for sidewalks or sewers were likely to be relatively sympathetic to *group* activities and claims. In contrast, those whose initial entry into community affairs was through appointive or even elective office (as members of the planning commission, advisory boards, or the council itself) were probably more "service oriented" and less sympathetic to the idea of a group struggle. The distinction is one which we have made earlier: the view of local politics as bargaining versus the concept of local politics as "managing" or administering a public business on behalf of the citizenry. The present hypothesis is that the Pluralist role orientation is likely to emerge from an interest-oriented recruitment context, while the Tolerant and Antagonist orientations follow naturally from a more service-oriented background. Table 4–7 presents the data.

Table 4–7 clearly indicates that Pluralists are more likely to emerge from group-oriented recruitment experiences than from more traditional community activities. Antagonists and to a lesser extent Tolerants are more likely to reach the council via appointive or elective office. A fair number, in fact, *began* their involvement in community affairs with their initial election or appointment to the council. It is also noteworthy that only a handful of councilmen mentioned partisan activity—an indication of the relative insulation, at least in terms of political recruitment, of nonpartisan from partisan politics in the San Francisco Bay Area.[9]

This association between the Pluralist role orientation and

---

[9] We do not intend to imply, however, that partisan politics are completely irrelevant for these cities. On this subject, see Heinz Eulau, Betty H. Zisk, and Kenneth Prewitt, "Latent Partisanship in Non-Partisan Elections: Effects of Political Milieu and Mobilization," in M. Kent Jennings and L. Harmon Zeigler, eds., *The Electoral Process* (Englewood Cliffs, N.J.: Prentice-Hall, 1966), pp. 208–237.

Table 4–7
Relation Between Prior Community Activity
of Councilmen and Interest Group Role Orientation*
(by Percentage of Councilmen Mentioning Activity)†

	Prior Community Activity				
Interest Group Role Orientation	Interest articulation (N=132)	Partisan (N=28)	General civic (N=152)	Appointive office (N=192)	Elective office (N=23)
Pluralist	33%	29%	27%	24%	17.5%
Tolerant	61	64	66	68	65
Antagonist	6	7	7	8	17.5
	100%	100%	100%	100%	100%

* The question: "Before coming on the Council, had you held any other local government position, like school board or so?" Coding categories were: (1) interest articulation—reform movements, election campaigns, incorporation movement, work with ad hoc group; (2) partisan—activity in political party organization or club; (3) general civic—participation in Red Cross, Community Chest drive, etc.; involvement with Chamber of Commerce or service club; (4) – (5) appointive or elective office—includes Council, Planning Commission, School Committee, Citizens Advisory Committee, and the like.
† Total Ns are larger than the number of respondents because multiple responses were recorded.

group-related recruitment experiences is echoed in the more immediate context of the last council election. Less than half of all councilmen reported formal organizational support in their last campaign. Once again, the group-oriented Pluralists were those who emerged from campaigns that entailed organizational support. (See Table 4–8.)

We have seen that men who reach the city council by the arduous route of interest group activity or participation in local reform movements are more likely to become Pluralists than are those who reached the public eye by "mainstream" community services. We have also noted that those who rely on organizational support in their campaign for office are more prone than others to continue their close relationship with group spokesmen after attaining office. While we have found some relation between environmental factors and role orientations that might lead us to expect a more active group life and more Pluralists in large in-

Table 4–8
Relation Between Interest Group Support
in Last Campaign for Office
and Interest Group Role Orientation

	*Group Support in Last Campaign**		
Interest Group Role Orientation	Formal organizational support (N=181)	Informal support or unofficial help from individuals in group (N=48)	No support (N=178)
Pluralist	32%	22%	18%
Tolerant	62	69	73
Antagonist	6	9	9
	100%	100%	100%

* The question: "In your last campaign for the Council, were there any community groups or organizations which supported you?"

dustrial cities than in small residential communities, we are far from arguing a direct causal relationship between environment, group life, recruitment patterns, and group role orientations. Our data simply do not support such a view. What we *have* found is a pattern of relationships that seems to link, to a modest degree, the choice of the Pluralist orientation, certain personal characteristics (high education, youth, etc.), certain environmental factors (community size, industrialization, high education of citizens), and certain recruitment paths to the council (interest activity rather than service activity). We did *not* find—and indeed did not expect to find—that most or all councilmen in large cities are Pluralists or that most councilmen's campaigns in those cities are interest-based. We expected and found, instead, that *where* the environment is large and complex, and where campaigns are rooted in interest politics, we are more likely to find Pluralists in greater numbers than is the case in other political environments.

This pattern of variables associated with the Pluralist orientation leads us to speculate that while such an orientation may follow more logically from some combinations of personal, environmental, and recruitment backgrounds than from others, it is not the easiest or most natural orientation for councilmen to adopt. It may require a certain personal fortitude or indifference to the opinion of fellow incumbents that is not asked of councilmen who adopt roles more in tune with the traditional suburban (and even nonpartisan urban) ethos of managerial politics.

Some support for this reasoning is seen in Table 4–9, which links councilmen's statements concerning the effort put into their campaign for office to the choice of interest group role orientations.

Table 4–9
Relation Between Councilman's Effort in Campaigning and Interest Group Role Orientation

	Councilman's Estimate of Effort		
Interest Group Role Orientation	Hard campaign (N=200)	Some/not much effort (N=157)	No effort (N=35)
Pluralist	30%	20%	17%
Tolerant	64	74	69
Antagonist	6	6	14
	100%	100%	100%

Here we can see a clear relation between the necessity or choice to wage a hard campaign and the later adoption of the Pluralist orientation. We anticipate even stronger ties between the Pluralist role and the amount of effort a councilman must pour into the difficult tasks of acting as mediator both within the council itself and between councilmen and other community actors. We shall deal with these subjects in the next two chapters.

Chapter 5

Interest Group Role Orientations: Consequences for Bargaining Behavior Within the Council

In the preceding chapters we have completed two major tasks. We have divided councilmen into three types, in accordance with their differing orientations toward community interest spokesmen, and have demonstrated that this typology has considerable predictive capacity for a range of councilmen's perceptions, attitudes, and behavior toward groups. We then sought for some clues as to the *origins* of contrasting interest group role orientations. In the course of this search we found that certain characteristics of the cities in which councilmen operate and the paths toward public office which councilmen utilized were closely related to the group role orientations they adopted as councilmen.

We now approach the task of delineating some of the *consequences* of differing group role orientations, both for the internal functioning of the council and for the way in which councilmen relate to their constituents. In this chapter, we consider bargaining and voting patterns within the council; in the next chapter, we study representational and purposive roles, and councilmen's attitudes toward interest articulation structures other than local groups.

It is possible to distinguish between two diametrically opposed conceptions of local politics: the "political" and the "managerial" views. Those holding the managerial view are likely to view policy decisions as routine, consensual, and noncontroversial. Policy-making consists of a careful search for the right answer, or for "the public interest." Little or no conflict need arise if rational men conduct this search in a spirit of good will. The opposing, or political, view sees competition over relatively scarce resources as an integral part of the policy-making process. Policy-making consists, at least in part, of balancing conflicting claims on these resources. The public interest is the resultant of such balancing activity.

Few would argue that competition is the sum total of the political process. A great deal of political behavior, among both elected decision-makers and the electorate at large, can be and is consensual. Many legislative and administrative tasks are routine and noncontroversial; many legislative votes are unanimous *because* no competition arises from the matter at hand. The point is that some councilmen, citizens, and political philosophers talk as if *all* political decisions could be routine.

It does not matter for our purposes whether the sought-after "right answer" is conceived as the "General Will" or the proper "solution" according to principles of "scientific management." Both Rousseau and the scientific management school of public administration deny the necessity of conflict over a wide range of decisions involving the allocation of scarce resources.

This view is particularly tempting and common where reasonably small homogeneous populations are concerned. In a small, upper-class suburb, for example, once the notion of rational city planning is accepted and a well-trained city staff is hired, most public decisions can be made routine. The task of a councilman thus becomes one of general legislative oversight, public service, interpretation, and explanation. No bargaining, log-rolling, or adjudicating need be involved.

There is little doubt that it is easier to adopt and carry out the managerial view in some communities than in others. In large, heterogeneous cities—and in those where the population is large in relation to available tax resources—a clash of interests seems almost inevitable. We have shown earlier, however, that while there is a moderately strong relationship between the size and industrial complexity of cities and the choice of the Pluralist orientation, the "fit" is far from perfect. We argue analogously that the political conception of policy-making will not be confined to councilmen in large complex cities, nor will managerial councilmen emerge only in homogeneous suburbs. The choice of a group role orientation hinges in part on personal preferences and experiences, and general conceptions of politics probably depend as much on these experiences as they do on the environmental factors discussed.

We are now able to make some specific predictions about the relationship between interest group role orientations and these different conceptions of policy-making in the community. First, Pluralists will be far more likely than others to have what we have called a political conception of the local policy process. The Pluralist accepts (and welcomes) the idea of a group struggle; similarly, he is likely to accept the need for bargining at the council table. In addition he is more likely than others to exert himself in using his powers of persuasion to win over both his constituents and his fellow councilmen to his own views. He does not believe that most matters that enter into public debate are "routine." Nor does he believe that unanimity (on the council or among the constituency) is either the normal or desired state of affairs. Finally, he is probably less concerned with the substance of a political decision than he is with the general support given to that decision, and hence to its ultimate acceptability or "legitimacy."

The Antagonists and Tolerants are both likely to take the managerial view. They will look with suspicion or displeasure on the idea of bargaining. Log-rolling, *quid pro quo,* or persuasion which rests on pragmatic arguments, is considered to be "dirty politics." Unanimity is desirable, and given sufficient good will, backed by expert administrative advice, it is attainable even on controversial matters. The ultimate content of decisions, guided by principles of sound planning and administrative rationality, is more important than the support given to these decisions. An Antagonist or Tolerant will probably not lean over backwards to persuade his colleagues or constituents; his work is to plan, to protect, to solve the city's problems by going beyond the compromising or conciliatory level of building legislative alliances and placating outside interests.

Table 5–1 shows councilmen's attitudes toward the bargaining process within the council itself. As expected, those who perceive and approve of bargaining and alliance formation with outside organizations (the Pluralists) are also prone to see and favor the equivalent process among councilmen. Antagonists are more aware of council bargaining than are Tolerants, but they are equally likely to oppose this bargaining. Note, however, that Antagonists and Pluralists are equally likely to condemn bargaining but to favor "compromise." Apparently the idea of giving up a part of what one wants for the sake of agreement is acceptable for a significant portion of both Pluralists and Antagonists, whereas the idea of cold-blooded trading is not. The difference in terms of outcomes is unclear to the author, but it appears that councilmen are concerned with what seems to be a motivational distinction.

Finally, it is apparent that only a few councilmen approve of bargaining. In fact a majority of those who answered the attitudinal question believe that both bargaining and compromise are either unnecessary or undesirable aspects of legislative behavior. Pluralists are more likely to take the view that some bargaining and/or compromise is a necessary aspect of the local political process.

Table 5–2 shows councilmen's responses to a question about unanimity. Respondents were asked to indicate which statements on a seven-item checklist were "often relevant," "sometimes relevant," or "never relevant" reasons for unanimous votes on their own council. Five of these statements can readily be classified as either (1) implying an acceptance of *quid pro quo* activities and/or active efforts at reaching a private compromise, or (2) stressing the existence of, or need for, a basic consensus reached without manifest bargaining activity or compromise. Following the lines of our previous reasoning about the relation between group role orientations and acceptance of the idea of "trading off" or bargaining activity, we expect a relatively high degree of Plural-

Table 5–1
Relation Between Interest Group Role Orientation and Attitudes Toward Bargaining on Council

	Interest Group Role Orientation		
	Pluralist	Tolerant	Antagonist
Does bargaining occur on the council?*	(N=99)	(N=279)	(N=30)
Yes responses	46%	26%	33%
Respondents' opinion of the *amount* of bargaining that takes place:†	(N=99)	(N=279)	(N=30)
Just right or too little	32%	17%	17%
Too much	7	4	7
No bargaining/no answer	61	79	76
Respondents' general attitudes toward bargaining:‡	(N=82)	(N=204)	(N=23)
Bargaining is good	24%	17%	4%
Bargaining is a necessary evil	17	12	9
Bargaining is bad but compromise is good	22	11	22
Bargaining is unnecessary or evil	37	60	65

* The question: "City councilmen sometimes talk about decisions in terms of bargaining—do you think this goes on in your council?"
† The question: "In general, do you think there is too much bargaining going on, too little, or is it just right?"
‡ Coded from general comments made in response to previous questions and to probes: (IF YES) "Could you explain a bit what this bargaining implies? Just what does one do in bargaining?" (IF NO) "If there is no bargaining, what other ways are there to make decisions?"

ist agreement with the first category of statements and a relatively low acceptance of the second.

Table 5–2 confirms this. Nearly half of the Pluralists acknowledge the need to support others in return for help on their own projects. At the other extreme, less than one-quarter of the Antagonists accept these statements. In addition, Pluralists are con-

Table 5–2
Relation Between Interest Group Role Orientation and Explanations of Council Unanimity

Statements on Unanimity (percentages indicate response of "often relevant" or "sometimes relevant")	*Interest Group Role Orientation*		
	Pluralist (N=78)*	Tolerant (N=242)	Antagonist (N=22)
Statements implying acceptance of idea of *quid pro quo* or compromise:			
"We go along with others to get support for our own proposals."	42%	32%	23%
"We try to iron out differences in private, before the issue comes up in open sessions."	53	48	32
Statements ignoring idea of compromise or stressing need for or existence of *consensus*:			
"We just don't like to disagree wherever possible."	33	49	45
"There is an unwritten rule that it is better to agree than to disagree."	8	14	18
"There is simply no disagreement on many issues."	83	92	90

* Number of respondents equals the number answering the most-frequently-answered question. "No answers" on other statements were counted as "never relevant" on the theory that those who checked some but not all statements believed the statements they ignored to be unimportant. The remaining two statements on the list failed to discriminate because of overwhelming agreement or disagreement. These were "We usually talk an issue over and try to reach agreement" (95% agreed) and "You go along with others even if you disagree a bit because it is uncomfortable to be in the minority" (12% agreed).

siderably more likely than the others to agree that efforts to reach a private compromise are important to the council. The fact that almost half of our respondents found this statement relevant is especially interesting in light of California's "Brown Act," which forbids closed or private council meetings except on personnel matters. Apparently the need for private consensus exceeds the wish that councilmen might have to observe the spirit of the legal requirement for public debate.[1]

A similar pattern of responses is evident on statements implying the existence and desirability of consensus without bargaining. Pluralists are consistently less likely than others to explain unanimity in terms of either natural consensus ("There is simply no disagreement . . .") or conscious efforts at consensus ("We just don't like . . . ," "There is an unwritten rule . . ."). Again, the total pattern of responses is interesting: the overwhelming majority of councilmen believe that a natural consensus exists and, at the same time, less than a majority accept the idea of a conscious effort to reach agreement, at least in the abstract.

The picture that emerges from this combination of responses to all five statements is one of councils in which:

1. little disagreement exists on many issues;
2. when the possibility of disagreement arises, it is disliked—attempts are made by many councilmen to prevent council squabbles from reaching the public eye;
3. yet there is no norm against open disagreement, and trading off is not considered an acceptable way to promote unanimity.

This composite picture is somewhat inconsistent in regard to the presumably narrow area where a high potential for disagreement exists. How are public debates and split votes prevented if there are no formal or informal mechanisms (e.g., rules of the game, or bargaining techniques) for reaching consensus? One possible explanation is that there is, in fact, a considerable amount of tacit bargaining taking place among these councilmen. If we accept this explanation, then it appears that most Pluralists accept and recognize the idea of tacit bargaining; in contrast, their fellow

---

[1] Much of this private ironing out of differences is likely to take place informally. Councilmen regularly get together for drinks after the council meeting in one city—a perfect setting for compromise and conciliation.

incumbents may not view an informal and indirect "feeling out" of others as an effort to compromise, trade, or bargain.[2]

Another plausible explanation of this seeming inconsistency hinges on the mixture of "is" and "ought" statements in the seven-item list to which councilmen were responding. It is possible that the *wish* not to disagree in public, or the wish to avoid a trading-off process, was uppermost in many respondents' minds, and that these answers should be viewed as aspirations and norms rather than as descriptions of concrete council activities.

One indirect, although not entirely satisfactory, check on this question is available. Councilmen were asked how often they voted against the majority of the council, choosing between "often," "sometimes," "rarely," and "never." If we assume that councilmen who report that they "never" vote against the majority of the council either attempt to avoid public dissensus or are members of councils where *in fact* little disagreement arises, we would expect a high proportion of Antagonists and a low proportion of Pluralists in this category. Table 5–3 shows that this is the case.

There are two problems with using these data to answer the question of whether efforts to avoid public disagreement are in fact made by councilmen, and if so, whether differences emerge between the three types of councilmen. The first is the question of the differences in Table 5–3. While a strong contrast between Pluralists and Antagonists is evident in regard to the "never" responses, the trend is reversed for the "rarely" responses, and there is no difference between the three types in regard to "often" and "sometimes."

The second question is conceptual: Can we indeed assume that frequency of votes against the council majority is a valid measure for public disagreement? Many councilmen may answer "rarely" or "never" not because the council seldom splits but because they are themselves part of a relatively stable majority.

---

[2] There may also have been a problem with some of the statements on the checklist concerning unanimity. Some councilmen had difficulty with the phrase "rules of the game" in another part of the interview, interpreting the term in a very literal sense.

Table 5–3
Relation Between Interest Group Role Orientation and Frequency with Which Councilmen Vote Against Council Majority

Frequency of Vote Against Majority	Interest Group Role Orientation: Pluralist (N=98)	Tolerant (N=264)	Antagonist (N=27)
Never	23%	26%	37%
Rarely	45	41	30
Often/sometimes	32	33	33
	100%	100%	100%

Thus all that we can infer with any degree of confidence is the fact that relatively few Pluralists find themselves in the fortunate position of always being on the winning side.

One final aspect of councilmen's behavior might help round out this picture of the relationship between general conceptions of politics and interest group role orientations. How do individual councilmen behave at those times when the council is split and tension is high? Are they active in resolving the conflict, or do they try to ignore it? Do they turn the situation to their own advantage, or are they primarily concerned with restoring harmony regardless of the substantive outcome?[3]

The Pluralist might be expected to take an active role in resolving a conflict. He is probably more likely than his fellows to seize an opportunity to further his own causes. He approves of bargaining and trade-offs, and although he dislikes public dissension, he is neither likely to sit passively by and await its disappearance nor prone to neglect a chance to gain a few votes. The Antagonist is more aware of the bargaining process than the Tolerant, but disapproves of bargaining per se. If his dislike of public conflict is stronger than his perception of a conflict situation as an opportunity, he will probably be passive; he is, however, cer-

[3] We realize that the choice of strategy may hinge on individual psychological characteristics of councilmen as well as on their general orientations toward community policy-making.

tainly more likely than the Tolerant to perceive and use such an opportunity. The Tolerant, we would argue, is least likely to pursue his own policy goals in such a situation; he is likely to take either a passive, wait-it-out approach or a business as usual approach.

Table 5–4 presents the responses of councilmen to a question posing this situation. The hypothetical choices, in response to the question, are placed in the table in the descending order of opportunism discussed above. On the whole, our expectations are confirmed. The Pluralists and Antagonists are equally likely to use a conflict situation to further their own ends, while fewer Tolerants choose this alternative. Tolerants seem to prefer a business as usual approach, reminding others to get on with the Council's business—a tactic also used by Pluralists, but uncommon for the Antagonists. Antagonists are most likely to remain passive, although it is not their preferred answer, while very few Pluralists adopt a wait-it-out stance. In short, Pluralist behavior in such a

Table 5–4

Relation Between Interest Group Role Orientation and Individual Behavior When Council Is Divided and Tense

"When the Council is divided and tempers seem to fly high, which of the following do you try to do (PLEASE CHECK ONLY ONE)?"	*Interest Group Role Orientation*		
	Pluralist (N=73)	Tolerant (N=231)	Antagonist (N=21)
a. try to form a working majority for own point of view	32%	24%	33%
b. remind others that we have a job to do	27	35	10
c. try to calm with light remark or joke	29	26	29
d. sit back and wait till things calm down	12	16	29
	100%	101%*	101%*

* Discrepancies due to rounding.

situation is consistent with what we have termed the "political" conception of community politics, while Tolerants at the other extreme appear to be the least opportunistic of all councilmen.

Summary

In this and the preceding chapter we have highlighted several differences in both the environments within which councilmen operate and, more important, the career patterns which brought them into public office. We have argued that contrasting environmental and recruitment patterns have helped to produce, though by no means determine, differing interest group role orientations —and that the choice of a specific group role orientation implies in turn a differing conception of the policy-making process.

The councilman who has been involved in prior interest articulation activity is likely to approach even the low-keyed world of local nonpartisan government with a more bargaining-oriented stance than is the councilman whose previous experience has been limited in large part to a consensual apolitical "service-oriented" set of local activities. The first stages in the developmental sequence are unclear. Some men may have joined local protest movements or claims-presenting organizations *because* they conceive of local policy-making as a "political" process; others may have adopted this view as a result of their early experience in the recruitment process.

What is clear—and important for present purposes—is the consistent relationship between the choice of a Pluralist role and a more frequent political or bargaining orientation at the council table. We have used four measures for this orientation: (1) perception of, and attitudes toward, bargaining within the council; (2) frequency of voting against the council majority; (3) reasons given for unanimous council decisions; and (4) the ways in which councilmen deal with a tense public conflict within the council itself. In three of the four instances, Pluralist responses showed a strong trend in the predicted direction; in the fourth, the trend was mild, but was consistent with our expectations.

Thus Pluralists are more willing to admit that bargaining takes place on the council; others tend to deny that it happens. Pluralists are also more likely than their colleagues to believe that bargaining activities are at least a necessary evil if not a positive benefit. In addition, they attribute council unanimity not only to a lack of disagreement on many issues, a view widely shared by councilmen, but also to a conscious effort at trade-offs and/or an effort to prevent private disagreements from reaching the public eye.

Contrasts among different types of councilmen become somewhat more blurred in regard to the final measure: behavior in a stress situation on a split council. Pluralists, true to form, prefer to take an active role in resolving the problem and are quick to seize the opportunity to build a working majority for their own views. A very small number of Pluralists are passive in this situation. Antagonists, however, are just as prone to make what we have termed an opportunistic response, though nearly as many (almost one-third in each case) adopt a wait-it-out stance.

We are not surprised at this pattern, given the three elements which went into our basic typology. Both Pluralists and Antagonists are "group sophisticates." The major distinction between the two categories of actors is their attitude toward interest-based politics. The Pluralist sees and *accepts* what the Antagonist sees and *rejects;* in contrast, the Tolerant does not see and, for the most part, either accepts in a neutral fashion or takes a more active stance without ever being fully aware of what it is that he is accepting or rejecting.

We can thus anticipate and find a consistent Pluralist-Tolerant-Antagonist trend on attitudinal questions; measures of behavior, in contrast, may often show the Pluralists and Antagonists acting in a very similar fashion. Some Antagonists avoid group alliances because they disapprove of the efforts of "selfish" organizations to influence council policy. This behavior in regard to groups does not of necessity imply an avoidance of their own alliance-building efforts within the council, presumably in the name of the "good of the community." Nor does it preclude a receptive attitude toward interaction with prominent *individuals* outside of the council, who may be perceived by Antagonists as very important to the policy-making process. The crucial distinction is probably the aura of "disinterest" which such councilmen can impute to their own and such individuals' activity.

Chapter 6

Interest Group Role Orientations: Further Consequences

Differing interest group role orientations imply, as we have seen, contrasting conceptions of the political process in local communities: those who value a conflict of interests among groups outside the city council are likely to accept the idea of conflict and negotiation within the council. Do contrasting role orientations also imply differing attitudes and orientations toward others (besides group spokesmen) who make claims on public resources? Does the choice of a particular interest group role orientation imply a preference for either specific representational styles or specific purposive role orientations?

We shall answer these questions in the present chapter as a first step in dealing with a central problem: *What difference* does the choice of an interest group role orientation make in the way in which a councilman operates as a public policy-maker?

Orientations Toward Alternative Interest Articulation Structures

A variety of potential interest articulation structures exist in even the smallest and most intimate community. Interest groups, community influentials, the press, the city staff, and political parties are probably the most important in the towns and cities described in this study. In all likelihood, major differences between political systems arise not only from the presence or absence of specific interests and the resources for which these interests are competing, but also from variations in the structures which articulate those interests. We examine here the relationship between interest group role orientations and attitudes of councilmen toward two of these structures: community influentials and the press.[1]

We pose several questions. As far as individual councilmen are concerned, are interest groups, influentials, and the press mutually exclusive *alternatives* or are they *supplementary* sources of claims-presentation? Do Antagonists and Tolerants generalize their rejection or neutrality toward interest groups to community influentials and the press, or do they rely heavily on these alternative structures because they have insulated themselves from group claims? Similarly, does Pluralist reliance on interest groups imply indifference to alternative structures, or is accessibility to groups a part of a generally receptive orientation to all structures articulating claims?

If we are correct in reasoning that group role orientations are associated with a more general attribute—the conception of the local political process as "managerial" or "political"—we would expect orientations toward other interest articulation structures to parallel group role orientations. Councilmen who reject the claims of those who "have an ax to grind" are likely to be as unresponsive to individuals as to groups. Those who value testimony of group spokesmen because it helps clarify their own views are likely to welcome an exchange of views with individuals as well. A distinction needs to be made, however, between the respondents' perception of groups and individuals as interest articulators and their perception of these as interest *aggregators*.

Some Pluralists made such statements as:

> When groups have decided on a position one can assume that the

[1] Most television in the area originates in San Francisco (or in the studios of national networks with which several local stations are affiliated). Only a handful of cities have independent TV or radio stations that devote much attention to local political news. Thus, with few exceptions, radio and TV are not important for the present analysis.

> membership of the group has participated and thus a substantial number of people have the same position on the issue. I feel this is valuable. We have to get people to agree.

Antagonists appear to be equally aware of this aggregation function:

> I don't trust points of view formed by small groups without open hearings and the other side being represented.

Thus the question must be asked whether community influentials are also seen as playing a major role in aggregation, that is, in mobilizing community support and in narrowing the choice of policy alternatives, or whether this interest aggregation function is perceived as unique to community groups.

Orientations Toward Community Influentials

The present research was not designed to study the wide range of problems to which students of community power address themselves. Questions on influentials in Bay Area cities were included not in order to analyze in detail the structure of private power in these communities, but rather to round out the analysis of several sources of interest articulation. These were a series of nonpresumptive questions[2] concerning active and potential influentials who work through the council and other decision-making bodies. Table 6–1 summarizes councilmen's responses. Local businessmen and others whose salient affiliations are primarily economic are by far the most important individuals to councilmen. This finding is in striking contrast to the earlier low regard councilmen displayed for spokesmen of economic *organizations* other than the Chamber of Commerce. One plausible explanation is that businessmen are distrusted as organizational spokesmen because they are perceived in that capacity as pleaders for special interests; in contrast, they are trusted as individual tenders of advice because they are

---

[2] A presumptive question might take the form "Who runs things here?" For a discussion of bias attributable to research preconceptions on this subject see Raymond E. Wolfinger, "Reputation and Reality in the Study of Community Power," *American Sociological Review* 25 (1960): 636–644.

Table 6–1
Responses to Questions About Community Influentials*

Occupational or Organizational Affiliation of Influentials	Percentage of Responses
Economic or Organizational Affiliation:	(N=665 responses)†
Local businessmen, bankers, industrialists	27%
Realtors, developers, contractors	13.5
Organizational affiliation (mainly Chamber of Commerce, service clubs)	9
Alternate Articulation/Aggregation Structures:	
City officials outside council (judges, ex-councilmen)	28
Individual professionals (lawyers, doctors, etc.)	13.5
Press	6
Partisan officials	4
	100%
Reasons for Influence:	(N=473 responses)
Technical expertise, information	43%
Can mobilize support, has political experience or connections	26
General interest and activity in public affairs	14
Wealth, social standing	8.5
Stake in community (owns local business or large amount of property)	8.5
	100%

* The question was: "Are there any persons who are particularly influential here—I mean people whose voices are really important in council decisions affecting the city? Who are they . . . and what makes for his influence? What does he actually do to affect decisions made by the council?" Coders used councilmen's own terms quite literally in classifying occupational and organizational affiliations. Thus it is perfectly possible that a given influential is both a businessman and a Republican official—but the councilman's response was the guide to the coding.

† 385 councilmen answered the question (in addition to 21 respondents who named groups rather than individuals, and 6 who "didn't know"). The responses came from the 246 councilmen who named influentials.

seen in this capacity as relatively objective sources of technical expertise.

The final data in Table 6–1 lend only partial support to this view. Technical expertise is indeed the most prominent reason for individual influence, but the ability to mobilize support, i.e., to bring pressure on councilmen, is also cited by a very large number of councilmen. It is also interesting to note that about one-tenth of the responses fall into the classic "community power" reasons for influence: wealth and social standing.[3]

A slightly different approach to this question of individual influence can serve as a first step in analyzing the relationship between the group role orientation of councilmen and their attitudes toward community influentials. The prominence given to city officials and individual professionals, coupled with a relatively high emphasis on technical expertise, interest, and activity, led us to ask just what the term "influence" meant to our respondents. It seemed likely that there were two very different interpretations of the term: capacity to give advice versus ability to mobilize support.

When responses to the question "What makes for his influence?" were examined in this light, they fell into three categories (see Table 6–2). One type of response referred to influence in terms of advice-giving ability. For example:

> I would consult all four of these men on real estate problems; they're all active and involved in it, and I'd be sure of getting two different points of view.

Another councilman put it this way:

> These are all people I talk to on given problems. I don't ask anyone in general what I should do, but I've developed a list of about 18 people I consult regularly.

In marked contrast were the comments of councilmen who saw influentials as mobilizers of support. One respondent said bluntly:

---

[3] It is of course possible that those councilmen who mention general interest and activity in council affairs perceive such interest and activity on the part of wealthy or high-status citizens more readily than among others in the community. We have no evidence on this point, and we see no reason to assume that such is the case.

Table 6–2
Relation Between Interest Group Role Orientation and Definition of Community Influentials*

Definition	*Interest Group Role Orientation* Pluralist (N=58)	Tolerant (N=113)	Antagonist (N=15)
Influentials perceived only as advice givers	47%	61%	47%
Influentials seen both as advice givers and support-mobilizers	47	31	47
Influentials seen only as support-mobilizers	7	8	7

* The 216 respondents who perceive no influentials are not included in this table.

> I don't know of any hidden string pullers, but I think there are people who can help me get something through.

Another answered:

> The people who are important to a councilman are those who can and will influence other people during elections.

Finally, a number of respondents indicated a combination of these views: individuals are heeded both because they are well informed and because they can help sell council policies to the community.

> All of these men take an interest in the council, the planning commission, the school district. They attend work sessions, they keep abreast of what's happening. When a person does this you respect his opinions. If we are sound in our ideas or proposals, we can always get their support or help.

It can be seen that Tolerants are considerably more likely to perceive influence solely in terms of advice-giving than are Antagonists and Pluralists and that the response patterns of Antagonists and Pluralists are identical. At first glance, we have what appears to be another example of group sophistication: Antagonists and Pluralists are more likely than Tolerants to perceive an "objective strength" or "power" basis for individual influence as well as for group influence. It must be remembered, however, that the responses in Table 6–2 include only those councilmen who named influentials. Table 6–3, showing the relationship between group role orientations, number of influentials named, and the occupation or position of influentials, clarifies the situation.

Several trends are evident. Pluralists are more likely to name influentials as well as to name *more* individuals than do others; over half, in fact, name three or more. The typical Antagonist or Tolerant, in contrast, either sees no community influentials or attributes influence to one or two individuals. Second, and even more important for our purposes, Pluralists are far more likely than others to attribute influence to potential interest aggregators—men affiliated with business, local organizations, or the press. The Tolerant or Antagonist is likely to name individuals such as lawyers, judges, or city officials.

Once again we are painting with a broad stroke, but the differences between the three types of councilmen are entirely consistent with their group role orientations. Antagonists may be cognizant of the power potential of individual influence, but they clearly prefer individual or official mobilizers-of-support to organizational spokesmen. As usual, the Tolerants are the least cognizant of "significant others" outside the council and, like the Antagonists, prefer that those others operate as individuals.

One final set of data serves to confirm this interpretation. We see in Table 6–4 that Tolerants are the most concerned of all councilmen with technical information, expertise, and other "respect" characteristics of influentials. Pluralists are the most interested in the ability to mobilize community support behind a project. Antagonists, interestingly enough, place high emphasis on political experience and astuteness, a quality possessed by lawyers, judges, and current or former city officials. Information and expertise are clearly important to all councilmen. Beyond this, the basis for individual influence is very similar to the basis for group influence reported earlier, and the characteristic styles of Pluralists, Tolerants, and Antagonists remain consistent.

Table 6–3
Relation Between Interest Group Role Orientation
and Responses to Question About Influential Individuals

	Interest Group Role Orientation		
	Pluralist (N=98)	Tolerant (N=279)	Antagonist (N=29)
Number of Influentials Named:			
0	30%	51%	43%
1–2	17	21	28
3 or more	53	28	29
	100%	100%	100%
Occupation or Position of Influentials (by responses):			
Potential interest aggregation source:			
Businessman, banker, realtor, developer	47%	40%	35%
Organizational affiliation	14	7	7
Press, political party	6	10	9
	67%	57%	51%
Independent:			
City official, judge	19%	32%	27%
Lawyer or doctor	13	12	21
	32%	44%	48%

Attitudes Toward the Local Press

It is difficult to predict the relationship between interest group role orientations and attitudes toward the local press. While councilmen can pick and choose among both groups and individuals, in most cities there is only one newspaper that concerns itself with local affairs. Thus councilmen who in principle hold the printed word in high esteem may reject the editorials of the local newspaper because they support the viewpoint of the opposing council faction. Asking whether the local paper is useful may be equivalent to asking about the local Chamber of Com-

Table 6–4

Relation Between Interest Group Role Orientation and Perceived Bases of Individual Influence*

	Interest Group Role Orientation		
Basis of Influence	Pluralist (N=157)†	Tolerant (N=282)	Antagonist (N=34)
Information and expertise; other respect variables	50%	62%	44%
Political astuteness, experience in city government	15	10	24
Ability to mobilize support; connection with some part of public	16	13	6
Social standing or wealth	7	10	9
Economic position or stake in community	12	6	15
All other	0	0	3
	100%	101%‡	101%‡

* The question: see note to Table 6–1.
† Note that N refers to total responses, not number of respondents.
‡ Percentage totals more than 100% due to rounding.

merce: responses tell very little about general orientations to the press or to local organizations.

Nevertheless, we can state two general expectations: (1) Pluralists and Antagonists are probably more well read than Tolerants—they probably seek more, and a greater variety of, news sources than do the relatively low-keyed Tolerants; (2) Pluralists are probably more open than other councilmen to the *local* press as a source of information on constituency needs and community problems.

Table 6–5 shows councilmen's general newspaper reading habits. We note first that all councilmen read at least one daily or weekly newspaper and that the great majority read three or more. Pluralists and Antagonists, as expected, read more newspapers than do Tolerants and are somewhat more cosmopolitan in their tastes. Well over a third of the Antagonists go to the trouble to obtain

Table 6–5

Councilmen and the Press: Relation Between Interest Group Role Orientation and General Newspaper Reading Habits*

	Interest Group Role Orientation		
	Pluralist (N=68)	Tolerant (N=228)	Antagonist (N=21)
Number of Newspapers Read:			
1–2	35%	32%	24%
3	28	37	33
4 or more	37	31	43
	100%	100%	100%
Types of Newspapers Read:			
National/International	26%	15%	38%
Regional	96	89	100
Local	96	96	95

* The question: "What newspapers do you read regularly? (PLEASE LIST)." Responses were classified as follows:
(a) National/International: *New York Times, Wall Street Journal, Christian Science Monitor, Washington Post, London Times, Manchester Guardian,* etc.
(b) Regional: *San Francisco Chronicle, San Francisco Examiner, Oakland Tribune, San Jose Mercury, Sacramento Bee*
(c) Local: daily or weekly city and county newspapers, other than above (e.g., Palo Alto *Times,* Cupertino *Courier,* Burlingame *Greensheet*).

East Coast and/or British newspapers to supplement the coverage of national and international news provided by the *San Francisco Chronicle,* the most widely read regional paper in the area. It can also be seen that almost all councilmen attempt to keep up with local political news through a variety of daily and weekly community and county newspapers.

We shall report at a later point[4] that Pluralists are more likely than others to find value in the local letters-to-the-editors columns. It can be seen from Table 6–6 that a similar, but very weak, pattern pertains to the editorials in these papers. The most striking point about the table is the lack of difference in responses of the

[4] *See* Table 6–10, p. 102.

Table 6–6
Relation Between Interest Group Role Orientation and Attitudes Toward the Local Press*

	Interest Group Role Orientation		
	Pluralist (N=78)	Tolerant (N=242)	Antagonist (N=22)
Local Newspaper Is Read Regularly	95%	95%	91%
Usefulness of Local Editorials to Councilmen:			
Very useful	17%	15%	9%
Of some use	51	54	59
Not very useful/not at all useful	32	31	32
	100%	100%	100%
Perceived Local Newspaper Influence on "How This City Is Run":			
Much influence	15%	15%	14%
Some influence	42.5	45	45
Little/no influence	42.5	40	41
	100%	100%	100%

* The questions:
"How often do you read the local paper to see how council affairs are reported? (Regularly, occasionally, rarely, never)"
"How useful are the editorials to you? Are they—(very useful, of some use, not very useful, not useful at all?)"
"How much influence would you say the paper has on how this city is run? Has it (much influence, some influence, little influence, no influence?)"

three types of councilmen. At the same time, Pluralists are slightly more apt than others to find value in local editorials. We do not interpret this difference to mean that Pluralists and Tolerants who find editorials "very useful" are slavishly following a local editorial line in the policies they advocate. Here, as elsewhere, we assume that the press is valued for its information, in both senses emphasized by David Truman: technical expertise and, probably more important, a rough index to constituency demands and supports.

Up to this point we have found that Pluralists are consistently more open than others to outside influences of several types: local organizations, individual influentials, and (to a mild degree) the press. However, we have not asked which of these interest articulation structures is most important to Pluralists or to others. Our expectation is that organizational spokesmen are more important than are either the press or individuals for the Pluralists, since the prototype Pluralist has stressed not only interest articulation but interest aggregation as an important function played by organizations, and it is highly unlikely that either the press or unattached individuals can effectively undertake that task.

In contrast, the Antagonists probably value individuals most highly, since their objection to the selfish nature of group claims does not extend to individual businessmen, professionals, and local officials. We would assume that either the press or individuals are valued more by the Tolerants than are organizational spokesmen, given the Tolerants' lack of awareness of the bargaining process.

Councilmen's responses in Table 6–7 fulfill our expectations about the Pluralists, but this is not the case for the Tolerants. Both Pluralists and Tolerants value the information-giving potential of organization leaders markedly more than that of the press or individual influentials. In fact, organization leaders are important for more than twice as many Pluralists than is the press. In contrast, for Antagonists organization leaders are the *least* important of the three groupings, ranking behind both individuals and the press.

This pattern of responses leads to the inference that attitudes toward groups are crucial for the specific question asked. Councilmen who are at least neutral toward organizational activity value group spokesmen more than individuals or the press as purveyors of information. Councilmen who disapprove of group claims-presentation activity prefer to receive advice and information from other sources. The relative lack of salience of the group universe for the Tolerant apparently does not act as the strong restraint that the Antagonist's negative affect imposes on his interactions with group spokesmen.

In conclusion, we have found:

1. Pluralists are more open to alternative influence structures than other councilmen. Only one-quarter of the Pluralists, in contrast to about 40 percent of other councilmen, believe that there are no political influentials in their communities; Pluralists are also slightly more likely to value editorials in the local newspapers.

2. The three types of councilmen differ on the concentration of individual influence and on the bases for that influence. Only one or two men outside the council, according to Antagonists, have an important voice in city affairs; Pluralists report a more fragmented or pluralistic state of affairs; Tolerants are in mid-position. Pluralists are most likely to attribute influence to business spokesmen or other organizational leaders; Antagonists prefer past and present city officials and independent professionals. Pluralists and Antagonists are more likely than Tolerants to view individual influence as the ability to mobilize political support, as opposed to the

Table 6–7

Relation Between Interest Group Role Orientation and the Value of Three Interest Articulation Structures as Information Sources*

	Interest Group Role Orientation		
Responses of "Very Important" or "Important"	Pluralist (N=77)	Tolerant (N=235)	Antagonist (N=20)
Organization leaders in the community	87%	79%	40%
Influential individuals	56	50	50
Newspaper	41	49	45

* The question: "We are wondering from whom you get the best information about city affairs. Could you rank these items as to their importance? (PLEASE RANK FOR EACH AS YOU SEE FIT: very important, important, not very important, not important at all.) City manager or other city officials; other councilmen; people at council meetings; organizational leaders in the community; people in the city generally; the newspaper; people in the neighborhood; influential individuals."

An overwhelming majority of councilmen perceive the City Manager and city councilmen as very important or important; a relatively small proportion view people at council meetings, in the city generally, or neighbors, as important.

possession of expertise, although the latter capacity is of considerable importance to all councilmen.

3. For both Pluralists and Tolerants, organizational leaders are of more value as information-providers than are the press or individuals. For Antagonists, influentials and the press are more valuable than organizational spokesmen.

Representational Style

Up to this point, attention has been limited to the role orientations of councilmen toward relatively prominent "significant others" in the community. The next series of questions concerns a more diffuse role sector: the orientation of councilmen toward constituents and voters in general.

Wahlke and his associates found in their study of role orientations of state legislators that three representational styles could be distinguished: *Delegate,* the legislator who votes primarily on the basis of instructions from constituents; Burkean *Trustee,* the legislator who votes his conscience or convictions; and *Politico,* the legislator who consciously tries to reconcile his own judgment with the wishes of his constituents.[5] The question asked of state legislators was used in the present study as well. Responses of state legislators and city councilmen are compared in Table 6–8.

The almost identical distribution of city councilmen and state legislators in their choice among these three roles is striking. Still more surprising is the number of councilmen who feel able to play the Delegate role. Since councilmen are elected at large on a nonpartisan basis, they must rely on individuals and groups rather than upon clearly articulated party organizations for clues to constituency wishes. The Delegate role cannot be an easy one, yet 80 city councilmen prefer it to Burkean aloofness.

We would expect some continuity between group role orientation and representational style. We anticipate that Pluralists will make considerably more effort than others to seek out constituency views, or at least to balance those views against their own judg-

---

[5] Wahlke et al., *The Legislative System,* pp. 272–282 and *passim.*

Table 6–8
A Comparison of Representational Styles
of City Councilmen and State Legislators*

Representational Style	City Councilmen (N=434)	State Legislators (N=295)
Trustee (votes own conscience)	60%	61%
Politico (tries to reconcile own convictions with instructions)	22	25
Delegate (votes instructions)	18	14

* Based on responses to the question: "There are two main points of view on how a representative should act when he has to make up his mind: (a) One view is that he should always use his own judgment or follow his convictions and principles, regardless of what others want him to do. (b) The other view is that, being elected, he should always do what the voters want him to, even if it is counter to his own judgment or principles. I'm wondering how you feel about these different points of view?" The above tabulation of responses of state legislators was computed from Table 12–1, page 281, in Wahlke et al., *The Legislative System.*

ment. Pluralists are more apt to view the political process as weighing competing claims on the common resources. In addition, because paying attention to group claims may impress them as one means of ascertaining constituency wishes, they are more likely than other councilmen to believe that it is *possible* to play the role of Delegate or Politico.

Table 6–9 presents the data. A majority of Pluralists prefer the Delegate or Politico roles, while an even stronger majority of other councilmen choose to be Trustees.

There is very little evidence that those who act as Trustees find themselves in a position of conflict between their own and their constituents' wishes. Only a few Trustees mention a feeling of pressure from voters; most confine themselves to assertions like "This is what I was elected to do" or to complaints that voters are apathetic and uninformed. It appears that for these councilmen there is no real problem involved. Virtual representation, as defended by Burke, is the only option to which they give serious consideration.

This interpretation is supported by responses to several ques-

Table 6–9
Relation Between Interest Group Role Orientation and Representational Style*

	Interest Group Role Orientation		
Representational Style	Pluralist (N=100)	Tolerant (N=281)	Antagonist (N=30)
Trustee	48%	61%	63%
Politico	25	21	23
Delegate	27	17	13
	100%	99%†	99%†

* See Table 6–8 for the question on which representational roles are based.
† Discrepancies due to rounding.

tions about citizen interest and knowledgeability. It can be seen from Table 6–10 that most councilmen are skeptical about general civic interest and interest in specific elections. They also find little value in letters-to-the-editor on policy matters. Here, too, the usual sharp contrasts between Pluralists, Tolerants, and Antagonists emerge. Pluralists show considerably more faith in constituency involvement in civic affairs, and pay more attention to expressions of such interest, than do their fellow councilmen. Apparently Antagonists and Tolerants reject individual as well as group efforts to take an active role in the process of policy formation.

What effect does this differing sensitivity to claims presented by individuals and groups in the community have on the concrete *behavior* of councilmen? This involves two distinct phenomena: the way in which councilmen treat their constituents; and the way in which legislative orientations enter into the policy-making process. Two interview items are relevant to councilmen's behavior toward constituents. One deals with the amount of time and energy that legislators devote to the "errand boy" aspect of their jobs, while the other concerns councilmen's efforts to swing their constituents over to their own views.

Many constituents view errand boy functions as a crucial part of their representative's job. Such services may include providing information on a local code or ordinance, arranging an appoint-

Table 6–10
Relation Between Interest Group Role Orientation and Answers to Questions on Citizen Interest*

	Interest Group Role Orientation		
Responses†	Pluralist	Tolerant	Antagonist
1. Percentage of Rs who believe that citizen interest in council *activities* is "high"	29%	17%	13%
2. Percentage of Rs who perceive "much" citizen interest in council *elections*	53%	43%	23%
3. Percentage who pay attention "regularly" to letters-to-the-editors on city affairs	58%	48%	36%
4. Percentage who find letters-to-the-editors "very useful"	13%	9%	0%

* The questions:
1. "In general, how would you rate citizen interest in what the council is doing here in (city)? Would you say it is high, moderate, low, or non-existent?"
2. "How about the voters here in (city)? Would you say there is much interest in council elections, some interest, little interest, or no interest at all?"
3. "Do you pay much attention to 'letters-to-the-editor' on city matters? Do you do so regularly, occasionally, rarely, never?"
4. "How do you feel about these letters? Do you find them very useful? of some use? not very useful? not useful at all?"

† Number of respondents:
Question 1: P = 99, T = 278, A = 30
Question 2: P = 96, T = 272, A = 30
Question 3: P = 77, T = 240, A = 22
Question 4: P = 77, T = 238, A = 22

ment with a local or state administrator, obtaining civil service jobs, or advising on the draft and taxes. As Eulau points out, legislators are probably less favorably inclined than their clientele toward these service functions. Indeed, only about a quarter of the state representatives he studied mentioned the task spontaneously in their interviews.[6]

The errand boy function should be less necessary to the constituents of councilmen than to those of the state or national legislator. The city manager and staff are likely to be quite visible, even in a fair-sized city. Information on local ordinances or on the requirements for obtaining a city job are as near as the telephone, or perhaps a short trip to the city hall. The city dweller, except in a very large metropolis, does not depend on his elected local representative as he does on his Washington representative for guidance through a bureaucratic morass. The Washington or state representative may be viewed as delegate-ombudsman-encyclopedia rolled into one. The councilman is more likely, in his constituents' eyes, to share this task with other local officials, friends, neighbors, and nearby lawyers.

Nevertheless, we anticipate some constituency demands on councilmen. Noisy municipal garbage collection in the early morning, confusing tax assessment practices, or the obscurity of zoning regulations will probably evoke a plea for advice and explanation. Some of these requests will undoubtedly go to the councilman.

If we are correct in the belief that councilmen's role orientations can serve as a reasonably accurate guide to their legislative behavior, we would assume that those councilmen who state that they are open to group claims and express a desire to follow constituency wishes will place themselves at the disposal of groups and individuals who request help. Conversely, a councilman who finds little value in group activity, perceives little citizen interest in public affairs, and chooses a Burkean representational role would seem highly unlikely to extend himself in response to citizen claims, requests, and arguments.

Table 6–11 presents responses to the question: "In your work as a councilman, do you spend a lot of time doing services for people—giving information, helping them with requests, and so on? or some time? or not much time?"

---

[6] In Wahlke et al., *The Legislative System*, pp. 304–305.

Table 6–11
Relation Between Interest Group Role Orientation
and Performance of Errand Boy Function

Time Spent "Doing Services for People"	*Interest Group Role Orientation*		
	Pluralist (N=100)	Tolerant (N=278)	Antagonist (N=30)
Lots	40%	33%	20%
Some	33	31	23
Not much/none	27	35	57
	100%	99%*	100%

* Discrepancies due to rounding.

It can be seen that Pluralists spend a great deal of their time in rendering routine services to their constituents, while the majority of Antagonists spare little or no energy for such tasks. It should be emphasized that we are now considering councilman/general constituent relations—"services for people"—not relations between councilmen and group spokesmen. The Antagonist and, to a lesser degree, the Tolerant simply do not see errand-running for constituents as an important part of the councilman's job.

The second question concerning councilmen's efforts to sell constituents on their own views raises a more complex set of issues. Kenneth Prewitt has pointed out[7] that the classic control of constituents over their elected representatives—the threat of defeat in a coming election—simply does not hold for most of the city councilmen in this study. Very few intend to remain in office for more than a few terms.[8] Most councilmen view their task as a relatively thankless community service rather than as an important life ambition and a means for personal gratification.

Is there any strong reason, then, for councilmen to make an active effort to "sell" their constituents on what they are doing? We would argue that there is. If local officials are genuinely inter-

[7] Kenneth Prewitt, "Political Ambitions, Volunteerism, and Electoral Accountability," *American Political Science Review* 64 (1970): 5–17.

[8] Ibid., p. 10.

ested in accomplishing specific programmatic objectives (e.g., putting the city on a sound financial basis, protecting it from commercial "encroachment," creating racial harmony), many of them are likely to feel that they must have some constituency support for their work. This is not to say that local legislators will feel unable to move without 100 percent (or even 51 percent) backing from the voters. It is to argue that no legislative body can operate indefinitely without at least a minimum of citizen acquiescence in its work. The more innovative and expensive the program, the more likely that this support is necessary. Thus quite apart from the occasional councilman's hope for re-election in a highly competitive atmosphere, the frequent hope to accomplish concrete goals for the city should imply at least a minor amount of time devoted to persuading, converting, or explaining policies to constituents. Table 6–12 examines this premise.

This table again demonstrates an important difference between Pluralists and others in their behavior toward constituents. Most councilmen make some effort to convince voters of the merits of their own views, probably for the reasons we have outlined. Pluralists are more apt to make the attempt. Furthermore, they are more inclined to make active efforts toward that end than are others. Their responses tend toward debate, argumentation, and search for a compromise. Antagonists, and to some extent Tolerants, prefer a passive stance, simply restating and justifying their own positions. They probably assume that this action is adequate for the accomplishment of their tasks and, if they wish it, their ultimate re-election.[9]

These data, like those in Table 6–11, demonstrate that there are important differences in the way in which councilmen treat their constituents, differences that can be predicted in part by sorting out councilmen according to their group orientations. Treating the Pluralists and Antagonists as polar opposites, we find that:

1. Pluralists are likely to make considerable effort to help their

---

[9] Eulau calls these passive efforts a "communications function" and the active efforts a "mentor function." He views both, along with "errand boy" functions, as service functions. See Wahlke et al., *The Legislative System,* pp. 304–308.

Table 6–12
Relation Between Interest Group Role Orientation and Efforts to Swing Constituents to Councilman's Viewpoint*

	Interest Group Role Orientation		
	Pluralist (N=96)	Tolerant (N=267)	Antagonist (N=27)
Percentage Who Try to Swing Constituents to Own View	92%	80%	81%
Techniques Used for Influencing Constituents (by total responses):			
Active Efforts			
argue with and try to convince critics	22%	21%	16%
debate, discuss, compromise	22	18	16
appear at public meetings, group meetings	3	4	4
	47%	43%	36%
Passive Efforts			
state own position and explain why others are wrong	47%	52%	64%
publicize own views through press, letters, etc.	2	1	0
	49%	53%	64%
All other	4%	4%	0%
Total	100%	100%	100%

* The question: "If you disagree with people on an issue before the Council, do you ever try to swing them over to your point of view?" (IF YES): "Just what do you do to swing them over?"

constituents, when requested, with the provision of information and small services. This is viewed as a normal part of the legislative task. Antagonists are less willing to expend their energies on these errand boy functions.

2. Only a small number of councilmen ignore the task of selling their constituents on their own (sometimes unpopular) views of public policy. The Pluralists, however, are likely to make an active attempt; Antagonists are more likely simply to state their preferences with little or no positive effort.

Interest group role orientations, legislative styles, and concrete behavior toward constituents all "hang together" in a consistent and logical fashion. One set of councilmen appears to respect and value group and constituency claims on policy matters and to devote a large amount of energy to seeking out views, helping with small needs, and convincing on issues. Another set of councilmen takes the opposite approach: individual and group claims are at best a nuisance and at worst pernicious, and as little time as possible is spent in responding to claims, requests, and criticism.

The next stage of the analysis is devoted to relating clientele orientations (roles toward groups, individuals, and constituents) to orientations involving legislative output. To do this, we examine one more role orientation: the purposive role, or a councilman's definition of his main task on the council. This analysis enables us to make preliminary statements about outputs of the legislative system.

Purposive Role Orientations

A political system has been defined, for purposes of this study, as a network of role relationships involving the allocation of limited resources. The task of those who make final decisions on legislative outputs can be divided, for analytical purposes, into two broad functions:

1. The *processing of claims* made on the system: the weighing of interests articulated by groups and individuals and those who have no spokesmen; the ordering, or aggregation, of those claims.
2. The *formation of decisions* that will enable the system to adapt and maintain itself in a changing environment.

The way in which interests are aggregated or ordered will in part determine the nature of the adaptation process; the policies chosen to facilitate this adaptation will help determine the future context in which claims are made.

In some political systems, the function of interest aggregation is performed through the assumption of party roles by legislators: elections are carried out on a partisan basis, the structure of the legislature is determined by party alignments, and individual actors take cues from parties as important reference groups. In other political systems, interest aggregation may be taken over by the executive. This may be handled either through the leadership functions of the chief executive or through the sensitivity of relatively autonomous administrators to cues from constituency groups.[10] In the nonpartisan setting of the present study, these channels are largely foreclosed.

For some councilmen, political parties may be important reference groups for decisions on those issues, such as urban renewal, where national or state party positions are relevant. On most issues with which the council deals, the national and state party organizations have no clearly defined position. In addition, most councilmen accept the informal norm, as well as the legal stricture, concerning nonpartisanship. With rare exceptions, council blocs do not follow party lines, even on a sub rosa basis.

The city staff may perform some aggregation activities by recommending alternatives on policies, especially in those communities where councilmen and the city manager share the view that this is an appropriate staff function. There is, nevertheless, no strong chief executive whose functions are equivalent to the President, a governor, or a regional bureau chief. It is therefore likely that interest aggregation activities will become a part of the functions performed by councilmen themselves as a part of their purposive roles.

Several questions in the interview dealt with councilmen's own views of their job. Respondents were asked to choose the one of

---

[10] The classic statement of this point is Friedrich's "law of anticipated reactions." See Carl J. Friedrich, "Public Policy and the Nature of Administrative Responsibility," in *Public Policy, 1940* (Cambridge: Harvard University Press, 1940), pp. 3–24.

three statements that best fitted their "own conception of the job." The roles described in these "job descriptions" can be termed Negotiator, Advocate, and Administrator. The Negotiator is a councilman who "should seek out the viewpoints of others—colleagues, city staff, community groups, or private individuals—debate and discuss the issues involved, and negotiate some agreement." It is clearly an aggregative role and, as such, likely to be preferred by Pluralists. Given the inclusion of staff and fellow councilmen in the list of those to be considered, we assume that many other councilmen will find this an important role as well. A great many elected local officials may view with disdain the views of "outside" groups and private individuals, but the councilman who can ignore views of local administrators and his own colleagues is considerably more rare.

The other two roles fall primarily into the decision-making category; the major contrast is the source of the program in question. The Advocate is "concerned with advocating new programs or revising existing policies" and then attempting to "sell" his colleagues; the Administrator takes a staff-formulated agenda as given, and chooses from the alternatives offered therein. In both cases, the stress is on policy-making per se rather than on the achievement of negotiated settlements. One implies the councilman's initiative; the other calls for a relatively dependent role in relation to the staff.

Given the part-time amateur status of city councilmen, we would expect the Administrator role to be more popular than that of Advocate or Negotiator, administration textbooks and theories of separation of powers notwithstanding. Searching out new alternatives in a near-vacuum, without relying on staff advice or consulting with inside and outside sources, is a demanding task. It is probably too much to ask of a political actor for whom rewards and sanctions are negligible.

The Antagonist in particular is likely to prefer the Administrator's role since the job description does not call for "selling" ideas to his colleagues—a task the pro-unanimity, antibargaining Antagonist shuns, and one which his high faith in the city staff should render unnecessary. In fact, the managerial approach to politics that seems to be characteristic of the Antagonist stance strongly implies that near-automatic decisions flow from good staff work and recommendations.

Table 6–13 presents the data. We find that Pluralists do show a marked preference for the Negotiator style, both in comparison with others and in absolute numbers. More significantly, about two-thirds of all our respondents prefer this style. Regardless of the effort involved, and despite private qualms about negotiation and bargaining, most councilmen seem to recognize that an effort must be made to determine policies acceptable to both the political stratum and "significant others" from their constituency.

Antagonists alone fail to cast a majority vote for this style. A sizeable percentage opt for the Administrator description. We have thus found a strong indication of a rudimentary division of labor among councilmen. Those attuned to interest articulation activities in the community see their jobs primarily in terms of interest aggregation; those taking an antibargaining or managerial view are more often directly concerned with the final stages of the decision-making process and prefer a somewhat more passive style.

We turn next to a broad and basic question concerning purposive orientations. Respondents were asked, early in the interviews: "First of all, how would you describe the job of being a councilman—what are the most important things you should do as a councilman?" Responses were classified into six main categories, allowing for several categories per respondent. Two relate to interest aggregation and four to the later stages of the policy-formation process. The interest aggregation functions are:

1. *Tribune*: representation is at the heart of this response—consider or get a feeling for what people want, listen to constituents, listen to groups.

   Example:

   The most important thing is to represent all the people of the city. If you do that you've done about everything, and it's hard to do.

2. *Broker*: the classical "political" response in which the councilman sees himself as "middleman"—hear all sides, listen, act as liaison, act on behalf of all interests.

Table 6–13
Relation Between Interest Group Role Orientation and Self-Conception of Councilman's Job*

	Interest Group Role Orientation		
Job Description	Pluralist (N=76)	Tolerant (N=234)	Antagonist (N=22)
Negotiator style (seek out views of others, debate, negotiate)	71%	61%	45%
Advocate style (advocate new programs, sell them)	17	14	19
Administrator style (consider proposals of staff and experts; accept, reject, amend)	12	25	36
	100%	100%	100%

* The question: "Here are some statements that may pertain to the job of City Councilman. Which of these statements seems to fit best your own conception of the job? (PLEASE READ AND CHECK ONE).

a. The Councilman should primarily consider proposals and requests by the city staff or other specialists, and then accept, reject or amend these proposals or requests.
b. The Councilman should primarily be concerned with advocating new programs or revising existing policies, and try to "sell" his ideas to his fellow councilmen.
c. The Councilman should seek out the viewpoints of others—colleagues, city staff, community groups or private individuals, debate and discuss the issues involved and negotiate some agreement."

> *Examples*:
>
> I feel that all councilmen share the responsibility of finding a way through the controversies so that we can act in the necessary and responsible ways.
>
> The council is like a coat of oil between irate citizens and the city staff.

These orientations are not mutually exclusive. While the Tribune is primarily interested in *representing* public opinion, in both its concentrated and fragmented forms, the Broker is concerned with *conflict management* and resolution. Hence the Broker is more likely to view conflict as both inevitable and functional.

Table 6–14 outlines the broad differences between Pluralists and Antagonists: Pluralists are more likely than Antagonists to mention an interest aggregation role. Specifically, the high Pluralist emphasis on interest aggregation roles contrasts sharply with their fellow councilmen and is the most striking aspect of the data. This finding is consistent with the generally more receptive orientation of Pluralists toward all clientele groups.

As expected, the Tribune role is markedly more popular than that of Broker: nearly half of our respondents selected this role, in contrast to one out of five who chose to be Brokers. This preference may stem from the difficulties inherent in the Broker's role. Even a Trustee or a Politico can consistently act as a Tribune, *speaking for* constituency differences or views, rather than *mediating* between opposing sides, or between a council position and an outside stance. Moreover, mediation implies the existence of at least two concrete policy alternatives, which may not be the case. Local organization leaders, lone influentials, and others may frequently apprise councilmen of their wants and needs without posing an alternative that would necessitate mediation. There may simply be little need for the Broker's role between councilmen and outsiders.

In any case, data on council task-orientations on this point show that a sizeable minority of our respondents take no aggregative role, and that among those who do, the Tribune role is preferred.

The four purposive orientations arising from the second legislative task—making decisions that will enable the political system to adapt to a changing environment—are:

1. *Ritualist*: a procedural, relatively apolitical response emphasizing the conduct of routine business—gathering information, attending work sessions and committee meetings.

   Example:

   You have to do a lot of reading and study to broaden your background. You have to pay attention at council meetings.

2. *Director*: a nonpolitical response stressing direction or leadership, in a businesslike sense.

Table 6–14
Relation Between Interest Group Role Orientation and Purposive Roles: Interest Aggregation Roles*

	Interest Group Role Orientation		
Purposive Role Orientation	Pluralist (N=99)	Tolerant (N=282)	Antagonist (N=30)
Tribune and/or Broker role mentioned	65%	60%	50%
No mention of either Tribune or Broker role†	35	40	50
Mentions Tribune role	56%	48%	37%
Mentions Broker role	20	20	13

* The question: "First of all, how would you describe the job of being a councilman—what are the most important things you should do as a councilman?"

† These respondents did, however, mention at least one adaptive or maintenance role.

Example:

I would compare the Council to a corporate board of directors. We are responsible for all policy and fiscal decisions.

3. *Guardian*: a response concerned with preservation and/or protection of the community.

   Example:

   We are here to keep the city the way it is, a clean, residential suburb.

4. *Planner*: a response looking to the future of the community.

   Example:

   The most important thing is to evaluate the problems facing a city. You've got to keep ahead all the time to try to establish the future policy with the needs of the community in mind. Your job is to set policy for the development, growth, and well-being of the city.

Except for the Guardian and Planner roles, these orientations are not mutually exclusive. Performance as a Ritualist, for example, may be means to the ends pursued by a Director or Guardian. It is likely, though, that the Planner maintains a more self-consciously adaptive view, forming policies that will solve present or future problems. Both the Ritualist and the Director are likely to focus on routine, but neither sees policy-making in a problem-oriented fashion, as do the Guardian and the Planner. For the Director, if sound business practices are used as a guideline for council action, no problems need arise. For the Ritualist, however, the guide for decision-making is neither adaptation or maintenance nor the imperative of sound management; he may either perceive the whole job of policy-making as simple routine (passing laws), or he may conceive of his job as consisting largely of finding measures to meet the demands of constituents.

Table 6–15 shows the relation between interest group roles of councilmen and their preferences among these purposive roles. The most striking feature of the table is the lack of sharp differences between the three types of councilmen. Almost every councilman mentions at least one adaptive or maintenance role. The most common role is that of Ritualist, mentioned by almost two-thirds of the respondents; the Director role is preferred by well over a third of the councilmen; the Planner and Guardian roles are least popular.

The only strong contrast between Pluralists, Tolerants, and Antagonists occurs with regard to the unpopular roles: clearly the Antagonists are more attuned to the Planner and Guardian roles than others. In addition, Pluralists and Tolerants are a bit more likely to be Ritualists.

These differences, albeit limited ones, are suggestive because they are consistent with our conception of both the interest group role orientation and purposive role orientations. It is important to recall that a significantly greater proportion of Pluralists than Antagonists assume purposive roles that are aggregative. The Pluralist spends much of his energy on clientele relations. In adopting either the Tribune or Broker orientation (as well as the representational style of Delegate or Politico) he brings his claims-processing efforts to the council table itself. He has put his creative energy into his council work at an early point in the decision-making process. Thus he often approaches the council table believing that a solution inheres in the information he has gathered both on

Table 6–15
Relation Between Interest Group Role Orientation and Purposive Roles: Adaptive or Maintenance Roles*

Purposive Role Orientation	*Interest Group Role Orientation* Pluralist (N=99)	Tolerant (N=282)	Antagonist (N=30)
No mention of Ritualist, Director, Guardian, or Planner roles†	9%	9%	7%
One or more of these four roles mentioned	91	91	93
Mentions Ritualist role	65%	65%	60%
Mentions Director role	38	39	37
Mentions Planner role	12	11	17
Mentions Guardian role	13	11	23

* The question: see note for Table 6–14.
† These respondents did, however, mention at least one aggregative role.

the problem to be solved and on the line-up in the community.

The Antagonist, on the other hand, has tried to avoid interest groups. Insofar as he considers clientele demands relevant to his purpose as a councilman, and only half of the Antagonists do so, he sees himself as a Tribune-Trustee, speaking for rather than mediating between needs. He is a Trustee partly because he has little faith in the ability or interest of the electorate, and partly because he believes that it is his job, not theirs, to find solutions. The claims of groups and individuals, aside from a select few whom he considers expert, are distractions from the problem-solving task, and it is into this task that he, as a relatively independent actor, pours his creative energies.

The Tolerant is not so easy to describe. It is likely that some Tolerants stress the routine aspects of their task for the same reasons as Pluralists, for Tolerants are more likely to be Brokers and Politicos than are Antagonists. It is also likely that other Tolerants perceive little aside from the routine aspects of the council task. The Tolerant's indifference to bargaining processes and outside groups may be indicative of a general lack of awareness of the policy-making process, including a failure to see the need for a long-range view of council problem-solving efforts.

If our view of these relations between interest group role orientation, representational style, and purposive role orientations is correct, we may infer that some division of labor among councilmen takes place with regard to the handling of legislative problems. Claims are processed primarily by Pluralists, while new solutions are brought to the council table primarily by Antagonists. Tolerants and Pluralists share the routine tasks, while Tolerants and Antagonists share a concern that the city's business should be conducted efficiently, with an eye on the tax rate. This is not to say that Antagonists ignore claims or routine work, or that Pluralists are unconcerned about solutions for policy problems. Rather, the *focus* of attention for the different types of councilmen seems to vary in this way.

A series of questions can be raised in relation to this division of labor. In a legislative sytsem where a given role orientation, or cluster of orientations (e.g., Pluralist-Delegate-Broker-Ritualist or Antagonist-Trustee-Guardian), is dominant, are some legislative functions emphasized at the expense of others? If the Pluralist-Delegate-Broker-Ritualist orientation is dominant, and cues are taken largely from clientele groups, is the system slow to adapt to change? If so, is this lack of adaptation caused by councilmen sometimes overlooking possible new solutions which have not emerged from a clash of ideas between dominant groups in the community? If the Tolerant-Trustee-Director orientation is dominant, will both clientele claims and some new approaches to problem solving be ignored in favor of a low tax rate and a small city staff? If the Antagonist-Trustee-Planner orientation is dominant, will the claims of some clientele groups be ignored in the course of a search for long-range solutions?

Summary

In this chapter we have considered the relationship between councilmen's interest group role orientations and their orientations toward other interest articulation structures. We analyzed the relationship between interest articulation role orientations and orientations associated with two other role sectors: representational style (another clientele role) and purposive role orientations.

We have found that the interest group role orientation is a reflection of a more general orientation toward extra-council structures and clientele. Those councilmen who are most receptive to interest groups, the Pluralists, are also most receptive to their general clientele. They name more community influentials, and they rely more heavily on advice from such individuals than do other councilmen. They pay considerable attention to letters-to-the-editor in the local press, and they choose a representational style that attempts to consider constituency views in the course of reaching decisions on public policy. Antagonists and Tolerants, on the other hand, appear to be less responsive to extra-council influence both in regard to alternative interest articulation structures and their own representational style. Just as these councilmen resist or largely ignore group efforts to present claims, they also consider constituency views to be largely extraneous to the decision-making process.

Finally, we have found that the interest group role orientations of councilmen are related to two sets of purposive role orientations as follows:

1. Pluralists are more likely to play an interest aggregation role (Broker or Tribune) than are either Tolerants or Antagonists; the Tribune role is preferred to the Broker by the majority of councilmen who choose an interest aggregation role.

2. Antagonists are more likely to play the Guardian or Planner role than are either Tolerants or Pluralists; Tolerants and Pluralists show a slight preference for the Ritualist role. Almost all councilmen play at least one adaptive or maintenance role; the Ritualist role is preferred.

From these findings, we infer that some division of labor among councilmen takes place. Those who are most sensitive to clientele tend to put most of their energy into interest aggregation activities, while those who are most independent of clientele pour their creative efforts into the search for policy alternatives. One result of this division is a possible balance between the dual needs of any political system for claim processing and system adaptation.

Chapter 7

Councilmen, Community Interest Groups, and Policy Outputs[1]

In the preceding chapters no systematic effort has been made to take into account the material and human *environment* within which councils and groups operate, or to discuss the *outcomes* of councilmen/interest group relations. We turn now to this task, dealing for the first time with whole councils in relation to local interest groups rather than with individual role orientations.

A striking development in the study of urban and state politics is the effort of many scholars to link the content of public policies to the economic and political context in which those policies are made. A burgeoning number of studies have demonstrated, with near-unanimity, the intimate tie between socioeconomic variables like urbanization, industrialization, and population density and the amount of public expenditures for welfare, education, and general amenities. The allied effort to relate political variables such as party competition and voting participation rates to the level of expenditures has met with considerably less success. There seems to be only a slight link between party competition and public expenditures, for example, when socioeconomic factors are controlled.[2]

---

1 An earlier version of this chapter was included in Harlan Hahn, ed., *Urban Affairs Annual Review,* Vol. 6 (Beverly Hills: Sage, 1972).

2 See, among others, Dawson and Robinson, "Inter-Party Competition"; Dye,

There appears to be some hesitation about accepting these findings as final; the search for linkage variables continues, as do criticisms of the approach. There are at least three reasons for the persistence of the attempt to establish political "linkage":

1. The refusal of those who specialize in political analysis to believe that political processes or institutions are in themselves irrelevant to a central policy outcome—e.g., public expenditures.
2. The criticism, typified by Jacob and Lipsky's review article, that the most frequently used measures for economic inputs and for policy outputs have not been adequately thought out.[3]
3. Some dissatisfaction with what seems to be an ad hoc approach to questions of political linkage, and a growing realization that more effort must be devoted to theoretical questions if meaningful results are to be obtained.[4]

Jacob and Lipsky are primarily concerned with the question of validity. In what sense are measures of income or urbanization "inputs" into the political or economic system? They argue that

> . . . income, industrialization and education are not in themselves inputs. The measures have little relationship to the phenomena they are supposed to represent. We might conceive of them as environmental factors which might lead to the articulation of demands and supports and their communication to political authorities.[5]

None of these studies has, in fact, attempted to relate these "environmental factors" to measures of interest articulation or political communication. It was simply assumed that a high level

---

Politics, Economics and The Public; Hofferbert, "Public Policy and Structural and Environmental Variables"; and Ira Sharkansky, *Spending in the American States* (Chicago: Rand McNally, 1968).

[3] Jacob and Lipsky, "Outputs, Structure, and Power."

[4] Richard I. Hofferbert, "Elite Influence in State Policy Formation: A Model for Comparative Inquiry," *Polity* 2 (1970): 316–344; Guenther F. Schaefer and S. H. Rakoff, "Politics, Policy and Political Science: Theoretical Alternatives," *Politics and Society* 1 (1970): 51–74.

[5] Jacob and Lipsky, "Outputs, Structure, and Power," pp. 514–516.

of education or wealth in a given political community would automatically lead to a large volume of political demands. Several decades' work on this question has buttressed this assumption by demonstrating a correlation between both education and urbanization and adult membership in voluntary associations, levels of political information, political efficacy, etc.[6] But the link between potential for political participation and the act of formulating and communicating individual or organizational demands to public officials has yet to be demonstrated.

A second conceptual problem concerns the adequacy of commonly used indicators for government services. Measures of per capita expenditures, teacher/pupil ratios, and the like tell us very little about the distribution of benefits to different groupings of citizens. Differentials in such distribution may be far more important in their effect on those involved than the absolute or per capita amounts of those benefits and may be intimately tied to the demands made on the political system.

With regard to theoretical problems, recent studies imply that party competition and citizen turnout are important for expenditure policies, but in none of these studies is there an explicit attempt to include the idea of political competition or participation in a more general theory of politics. Competition and participation are important—somehow—but the precise fashion in which they relate to interest articulation or political communication or, more important, to the way in which policy-makers operate remains unspecified.

Two studies which depart from this pattern deserve attention. These are analyses by Prewitt and Eulau of the relationship between city size, community support, political recruitment patterns, and representational response style, and Eyestone's examination of policy outputs in relation to city characteristics and councilmen's policy preferences. Both studies rely on the same data from city councilmen in the San Francisco Bay Area as used in our own work (see Appendix A, p. 155).

[6] See, for example, Charles R. Wright and Herbert H. Hyman, "Voluntary Association Membership of American Adults: Evidence from National Sample Surveys," *American Sociological Review* 23 (1958): 284–294; and Almond and Verba, *The Civic Culture*, pp. 180–213, especially Figures 1 and 2.

City councils were found to be more responsive to interest groups and other attentive publics in large cities than in small communities. The size of cities (used as an indicator for social pluralism) is strongly related to the choice by councilmen of a representational style ranging from one that is highly responsive to attentive publics (in large cities) to one which is largely self-defined (in small cities).[7] Population density seems to be the single most important economic or social characteristic of cities for predicting municipal expenditure patterns. Yet decisions on amenities and planning expenditures are systematically related to the policy preferences of city councilmen as well as to demography.[8]

Prewitt, Eulau, and Eyestone have shown an important connection between some socioeconomic characteristics of the urban environment, the style and preferences of elected policy-makers, and the pattern of government expenditures. They have not, however, dealt with a related set of questions concerning what might be called "the demand environment" and the making of public policy. What difference, if any, does the quality of interest group activity make in the councilman's policy preferences? Does the councilman's concrete relations with local interest groups affect the policy choices he makes on public expenditures?

Theoretical Considerations and Research Indices

We are concerned with the manner in which environmental conditions such as industrialization and city size give rise to political demands, and how these demands are converted by policy-makers into policy outputs. The policy-making process in American cities (and in other political settings) can be described as a relationship between five sets of variables: environmental factors; the political translation process; the political conversion process;

[7] Kenneth Prewitt and Heinz Eulau, "Political Matrix and Political Representation: Prolegomenon to a New Departure from an Old Problem," *American Political Science Review* 63 (1969): 427–441.

[8] Robert Eyestone, *The Threads of Public Policy: A Study in Policy Leadership* (Indianapolis: Bobbs-Merrill, 1971).

policy outputs; and feedback (see Figure 7–1). Our main interest here is in the processes of translation and conversion: the way in which actors in a political setting come to make demands on public policy-makers; the choice of activities undertaken by organized interest groups; and the attitudes and behavior of policy-makers toward such organized groups.

A description of these sets of variables, together with the indices used in this study, may be helpful.

1. *Environmental factors.* Policy-making takes place within a relatively enduring material and human setting that may be viewed (depending on the research problem at hand) as either self-contained or permeable to inputs from outside.[9] Cities, for example, may be described in terms of climate, geographical location, size, population density, and land use. They may also be discussed in terms of human potential, i.e., educational and occupational skills, wealth, and the heterogeneity of the actors within the environment.

From the range of census indicators at hand, four environmental characteristics were chosen: city size, industrialization, education, and family income. The measures for these variables are city population (July 1965); the percentage of urbanized land in commercial or industrial use (July 1965); percentage of high school graduates among the adult population (1960); and median family income (1960). Size and industrialization should provide a strong indication of the political and social complexity of the cities in question (potential for demand articulation), while the other two indicators serve as measures of socioeconomic status (potential for participation).

Since these indicators are in common use, only a few explanatory comments are needed. Size and industrialization seem appropriate measures of what can be called potential for conflict over the disposition of community resources: the larger and more diverse the socioeconomic environment, the more likelihood of argument over the use of public goods. Similarly, high economic and educational

---

[9] For purposes of the present study we have ignored exogenous factors. We believe this is justified for the problem chosen.

Figure 7–1
The Urban Policy-Making Process

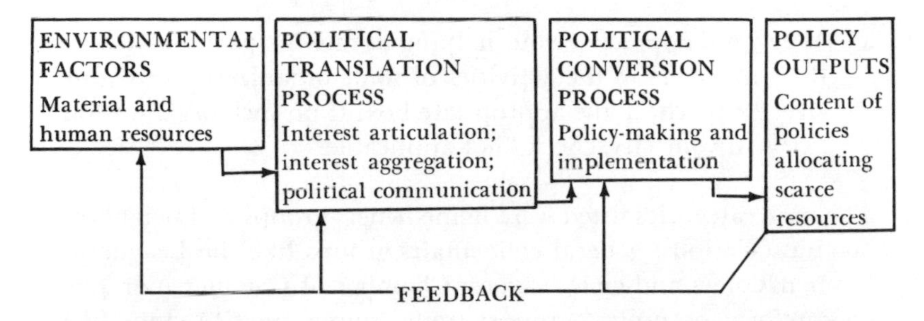

status are both potential political resources. Education is probably most directly related to the possession of the political skills, knowledge, and sense of efficacy of citizens that precede the decision to participate in urban affairs.[10]

2. *The political translation process.* How do actors formulate and communicate their demands and supports to policy-makers? How, if at all, are private needs, views, and supports translated into public questions? The vehicles for such a translation are likely to differ in a city from those in a nation or a state. Two obvious differences exist: the relatively greater intimacy and limited scope of urban government in comparison with the sovereign and usually more complex units of state and national government; and the nonpartisan legal structure of most local governments. These features of urban government imply a somewhat fragmented style of demand articulation and political communication. The fact of legal nonpartisanship leads us to look for linkage structures other than the political party, although as noted elsewhere, the phenomenon of "latent" partisanship alerts us to the continuing relevance of party identification and party activities for political campaigns in the local community.[11]

Information provided by our respondents was used to develop

---

[10] We have found, as have others, a strong relationship between the two pairs of variables: .36 for population and land in industrial use, and .72 for high school graduates and median family income. See Table 7–1, p. 130.

[11] See Eulau, Zisk, and Prewitt, "Latent Partisanship."

measures of local interest group activity.[12] Three questions were asked:

a. We would appreciate your helping us rate the participation of their members in the activities of some organizations in your city. Please check the appropriate box. If no such organization exists in your city, check "not applicable."

The nine categories listed were homeowners groups and neighborhood associations; general civic affairs groups like the League of Women Voters and civic leagues; Chamber of Commerce or Jaycees; reform or protest groups; trade unions; service clubs like Kiwanis or Rotary; merchants associations; political party clubs or organizations; garden clubs, trail clubs, and library associations. The checklist offered a choice between "high participation," "moderate participation," and "low participation."

b. Do any of the community groups or organizations ever contact you personally to seek your support?
c. In your last campaign for the council, were there any community groups or organizations which supported you? What kinds of things did they do?

Four different measures of group activity in each community were developed by aggregating the responses of all councilmen in a given city.[13] These measures are:

---

[12] This information is limited to 81 cities (as opposed to the 82 communities discussed in previous chapters) because of response failure in one city on questions regarding interest group *activities*. See Footnote 7 for Chapter 1 and Appendix A, p. 155.

[13] See Prewitt and Eulau, "Political Matrix and Political Representation," for a justification of aggregating councilmen's responses as measures of whole-city tendencies. We believe that this aggregation can be justified on yet another ground: the effect of several councilmen who are responsive to groups is likely to extend to the whole council, in terms of the degree to which group claims are considered or groups are brought into the decision-making process. Councilmen do not act as isolated individuals, and the fact that they act with regard to groups or others is likely to spill over into their colleagues' behavior.

Number of active groups: the mean number of groups rated as to members' participation (regardless of rating) out of the nine possible categories (53 percent of the council means were seven to nine groups; 47 percent fell below 7.0 groups.)

Intensity of group members' activity: average ranking of members' participation, computed by dividing total number of organizations whose members were "very active" or "active" by total that were ranked.

Political communications of groups to policy-makers: computed by percentage of councilmen who reported group contacts or requests for support.

Group activity in elections: computed by percentage of councilmen who reported *formal* group support in their last campaign for office.

3. *The political conversion process.* Almond and Powell refer to their six functions (interest articulation, interest aggregation, communications, legislation, administration, and adjudication) as "the *conversion processes* of the political system—the processes which transform the flow of *demands* and *supports* into the political system into a flow of extraction, regulation, distribution . . . ."[14] The term is used here in a more limited sense. It refers to the orientations and concrete behavior of policy-makers active in transforming (or in some cases, ignoring or refusing to transform) political demands and communications into policies.

A complete description of this process would include the orientations and behavior of policy-makers toward *all* "significant others": fellow policy-makers, the general public, and the large number of specialized organizations that participate in the prior process of political translation. We shall concentrate only on city councilmen's orientations and behavior toward community groups. Such a focus cannot give us a complete picture of the political conversion process, but groups seem an appropriate starting point

---

[14] Gabriel A. Almond and G. Bingham Powell, *Comparative Politics: A Developmental Approach* (Boston: Little, Brown and Company, 1968), p. 6. Emphasis in original.

because of their key role in the communication of community demands and supports.

For this purpose we use two measures: the extent to which councilmen seek group support on matters before the council, and the councilmen's interest group role orientations. The aggregate measure for both questions is simply, in one case, the percentage of Pluralists on a given council and, in the other, the percentage of councilmen who report seeking group support.

4. *Policy outputs* are the result of decisions and nondecisions concerning the allocation of public resources. Resources may be material (e.g., public funds and facilities), symbolic (e.g., public offices of an honorific nature), or as is frequently the case, they may combine material and symbolic elements.[15] Demands for the distribution and use of public resources usually exceed their availability, hence their relative scarcity. The most important decisions involving local resources are probably those concerned with public expenditures and land use, and those which affect the structure of the policy-making process itself, such as voting requirements and provisions for recall elections.

We use here three measures of policy outputs, all of which concern public expenditures: (a) per capita expenditures, 1966–67; (b) allocations to "amenities" as a percentage of operating expenses, 1966–67; and (c) planning expenditures as a percentage of "general government" expenses, 1966–67.

Amenities are defined as *optional* city services that go beyond such basic services as fire and police protection, sewerage and drainage, water, and other public utilities. They include parks and recreation facilities, libraries, and some health programs.

Planning expenditures are funds spent by planning commissions. Per capita expenditures were computed by dividing total expenditures by total city population.

We would have preferred to supplement these measures with several other output indicators, such as expenditures on education and welfare, or the frequency of amendments to the Master Plan, zoning variances, and the like. We are limited, however, to indices

---

[15] See Murray Edelman, *The Symbolic Uses of Politics* (Urbana: University of Illinois Press, 1964).

that are readily available for all communities. School districts in California, for example, are not contiguous with city boundaries; thus school expenditure figures are not suitable for our purposes. We will argue, however, that while the overall level of municipal expenditures is largely dependent on the total resources of a city (e.g., taxable property), the way in which these expenditures are apportioned among differing services hinges in part on the relation between councilmen and those constituents who are making demands. Thus the share of public funds devoted to amenities spending may be a very important clue to the quality of organized group life in a city, and the relationship between city councilmen and groups.

A summary statement of the theoretical linkage concepts discussed above, as well as the indicators used in this study, is given in Figure 7–2.

Hypotheses and Results

Relation Between Environmental Factors and the Political Translation Process

Large cities and *highly industrial cities* have a greater potential for citizen competition over the allocation of scarce resources than do small or primarily residential communities. Size is probably the more important of the two characteristics. It implies a social, racial, religious, and economic heterogeneity which is likely to give rise to an active and varied organizational life and a high volume of political communications from such groups.[16] Groups are also apt to perceive a high stake in the electoral process in large and heterogeneous communities, and thus become active in council elections. The individual citizen may have a greater incentive to join a politically active organization in a large city than he would in a small community, simply because such organizations are probably taken more seriously by policy-makers in a complex

---

[16] See Prewitt and Eulau, "Political Matrix and Political Representation," for further discussion of this point.

Figure 7–2

The Urban Political Process:
A Schematic Presentation with Brief Description of Indicators Used in This Study

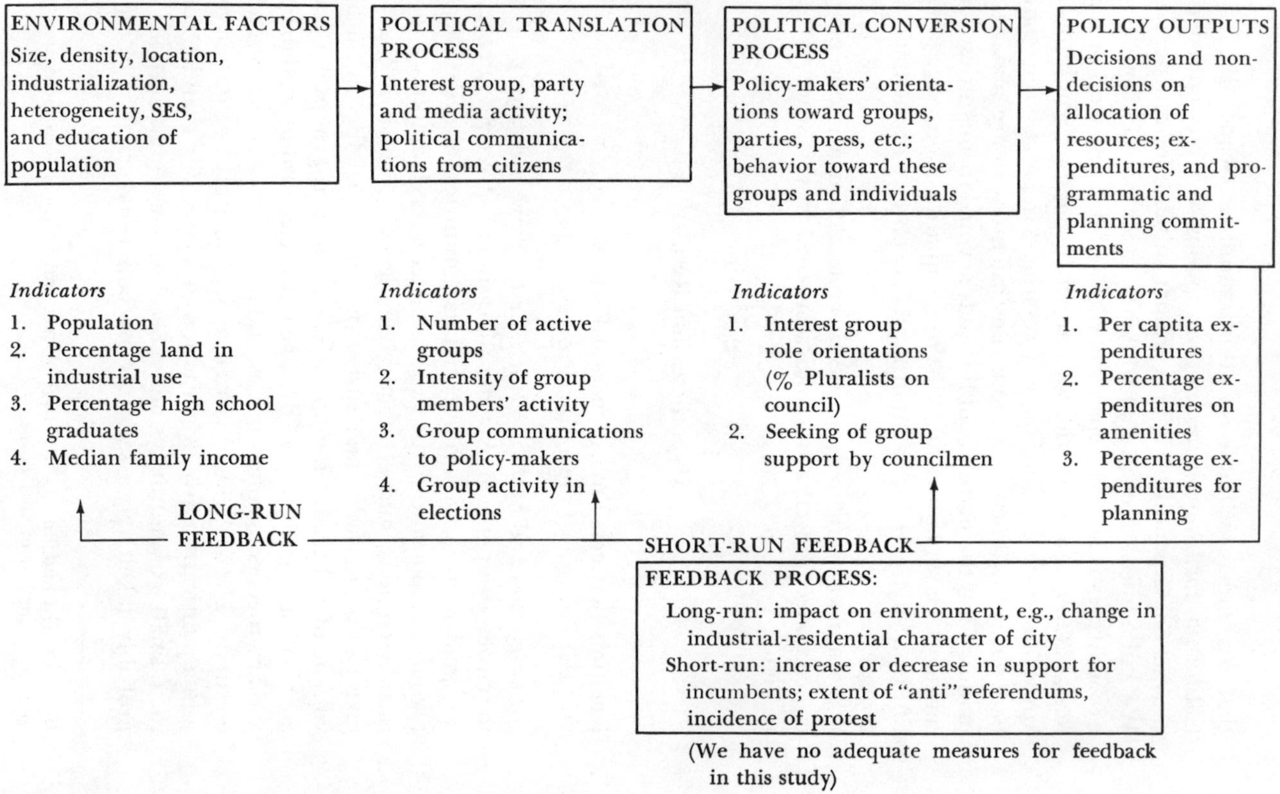

ENVIRONMENTAL FACTORS	POLITICAL TRANSLATION PROCESS	POLITICAL CONVERSION PROCESS	POLICY OUTPUTS
Size, density, location, industrialization, heterogeneity, SES, and education of population	Interest group, party and media activity; political communications from citizens	Policy-makers' orientations toward groups, parties, press, etc.; behavior toward these groups and individuals	Decisions and non-decisions on allocation of resources; expenditures, and programmatic and planning commitments
Indicators	*Indicators*	*Indicators*	*Indicators*
1. Population 2. Percentage land in industrial use 3. Percentage high school graduates 4. Median family income	1. Number of active groups 2. Intensity of group members' activity 3. Group communications to policy-makers 4. Group activity in elections	1. Interest group role orientations (% Pluralists on council) 2. Seeking of group support by councilmen	1. Per captita expenditures 2. Percentage expenditures on amenities 3. Percentage expenditures for planning

LONG-RUN FEEDBACK

SHORT-RUN FEEDBACK

FEEDBACK PROCESS:

Long-run: impact on environment, e.g., change in industrial-residential character of city

Short-run: increase or decrease in support for incumbents; extent of "anti" referendums, incidence of protest

(We have no adequate measures for feedback in this study)

urban environment. In an environment where the policy-maker is subject to a multitude of conflicting and often mutually exclusive demands from a variety of claimants, group claims may be given preferential treatment over individual claims simply because of the communications overload endured by the councilman. From the point of view of the local policy-maker, politically active groups in this setting may play a role in interest aggregation as well as interest articulation.

An educated and wealthy population probably possesses a greater degree of political skill and efficacy—i.e., potential for participation in group and other political activities—than does a poorly educated or low-income population. We would therefore anticipate a strong relationship between population characteristics and both the intensity of group members' participation in organizational activity and group utilization of local opportunities for political communication. We do not see any logical connection, though, between socioeconomic status (and educational skills) and the sheer *number* of groups that are active in politics, or group participation in council elections.

The information in Table 7–1 provides strong support for our expectations concerning city size and industrialization. There is a strong correlation between these characteristics of the urban environment and all four measures of group activity. Size appears to be a major determinant of the number of politically active groups. There also appears to be an unexpectedly strong relation between size and industrialization and the intensity of members' participation in organizational activities. One possible explanation for this finding is that a high stake in political outcomes in large, complex communities induces a heightened membership interest in group activity, just as it leads the organization itself to participate in local political campaigns.

There is very little relationship between income, education, and the political translation process. In the two cases where we expected to find strong links, only one—the tie between socioeconomic indicators and group communications—appeared, and even here the relationship is modest. In short, the potential for competition (implied by size and industrialization) appears to be markedly more important for the group life of these communities

Table 7–1
Relation Between Environmental Factors and the Political Translation Process

Variable A	Variable B	Correlation (Kendall's Tau B)	Significance
Population	Number of active groups	.52	.001
	Intensity of group members' activity	.27	.001
	Political communications of groups to policy-makers	.27	.001
	Group activity in elections	.19	.01
Percentage land in industrial use	Number of active groups	.20	.01
	Intensity of group members' activity	.28	.001
	Political communications of groups to policy-makers	.18	.05
	Group activity in elections	.25	.01
Percentage high school graduates	Number of active groups	.03	(NS)
	Intensity of group members' activity	–.02	(NS)
	Political communications of groups to policy-makers	.17	.05
	Group activity in elections	.04	(NS)
Median family income	Number of active groups	.05	(NS)
	Intensity of group members' activity	–.08	(NS)
	Political communications of groups to policy-makers	.19	.01
	Group activity in elections	.05	(NS)

Internal Consistency of Environmental Factors

Relation Between:		
Population and land in industrial use	.36	.001
Population and percentage high school graduates	.09	(NS)
Population and median family income	.09	(NS)
Land in industrial use and high school graduates	–.23	.01
Land in industrial use and median family income	–.06	(NS)
Percentage high school graduates and median family income	.72	.001

than is the potential for participation (implied by educational and income levels of the population). Income may have important effects on the local political process, but it does not appear to be significant for organizational activity, except in the case of political communication.[17]

Because of the very high correlation between median income and education levels, and the strong relation between city size and industrialization in these cities (see the last part of Table 7–1), partial correlations between the environmental and translation variables were computed, controlling for the remaining environmental factors. The relationship between city size and the translation variables remained strong throughout. Industrialization had almost no independent effect (apart from size) on the number of active groups and on the political communication process, but it remained important for both the intensity measure and the measure for group activity in elections.

Median family income is a markedly more important measure than education in relation to the political communication process. The relationship between political communications and level of education all but disappears when income level is controlled. The full data on partial correlations for the variables in Table 7–1 and subsequent tables are given in Appendix D.

To summarize: City size and, to a lesser degree, industrialization are positively related to four aspects of group life. The income level of the population is a good predictor for one of these aspects of group activity—political communications. The potential for competition and, to some extent, the potential for participation, as measured by three commonly used environmental factors, are related to the political translation process.[18] Thus, important links do exist between the first two stages in our partial model of the political process.

---

[17] It should also be noted that size and industrialization are genuine properties of the *cities* themselves, whereas educational and income measures are aggregated attributes of the citizens of these cities.

[18] It should be recalled again, however, that our measures for the political translation process are the existence of groups and the activities of groups *as perceived by city councilmen*.

Relation Between the Political Translation Process and the Political Conversion Process

We have been warned, again and again, not to assume that policy-makers' orientations and behavior will invariably mirror the human environment in which they operate.[19] To assume, for example, that all representatives in a business-dominated community will share and act upon the values of the business community is to accept a kind of representational determinism that is not supported by empirical evidence. Indeed, this lack of a perfect match between values of the representative and those he represents has been a common complaint of minority groups affronted by their seeming impotence.

At the same time, we suspect that the existence or the lack of a strong and diverse set of politically active organizations in a community will have some effect on the behavior of policy-making bodies. We do not expect a one-to-one relation—i.e., that all councilmen will be highly responsive in a city where local groups are well organized and active on political issues, or that no councilmen will heed group requests in a community where organizational activity is rare, sporadic, and poorly expressed. Nor do we expect councils to be pro-labor in a working-class community and pro-business in a high-SES city. Yet we do anticipate that policy-makers will be more responsive to group requests and more likely to form alliances with local organizations in communities where groups are highly organized than will be the case in those cities where groups are relatively quiescent.

We thus anticipate a high correlation between the political translation process and the conversion process. There will be more Pluralists and more councilmen who seek group help in cities where there are a large number of groups, many groups with intensely involved members, or groups active in both the political communications process and local political campaigns, than in cities where groups are less active.

---

19 See Prewitt and Eulau, "Political Matrix and Political Representation," and Hanna F. Pitkin, *The Concept of Representation* (Berkeley: University of California Press, 1967), on this point.

Table 7–2 confirms these expectations. All of the relationships expected are statistically significant, and with one exception (the correlation between the number of active groups and the extent of the Pluralist orientation), they are all strong. Councilmen in cities where groups are politically active are more likely to approve of group activity and to call upon groups for help on their own projects.

Partial correlations were computed (controlling for population) to test the possibility that a council's favorable stance toward groups might be attributable to the social complexity of the city rather than to the character of group life in that city. The relationship between the conversion and translation measures was weakened slightly as a result of this control, but remained significant in all but one case. This exception (see Appendix D) is the correlation between number of active groups and the extent of the Pluralist orientation: when population is controlled, the figure drops from .16 to .05. It is thus clear that the sheer number of organized groups has little independent effect on the councilman's outlook on group activity. What a group does carries far more weight than the simple fact of its existence.

One of the most interesting aspects of Table 7–2 is the contrast between the variables that measure *group activity* and those that measure *potential influence* in relation to the political conversion process. Campaign activity and group communications are more effective, per se, than sheer numbers or even membership commitment. This makes considerable sense if we believe that the attitudes and activities of policy-makers are in part a result of group actions rather than the reverse.

Relation Between the Political Conversion Process and Policy Outputs

Three general hypotheses concerning the relationship between the conversion process and policy outputs are proposed:

1. Levels of expenditure will probably vary with council orientations and behavior toward local groups, but will depend

Table 7–2
Relation Between Political Translation Process and Political Conversion Process

Variable A	Variable B	Correlation (Kendall's Tau B)	Significance
Number of active groups	Extent of Pluralist role orientation	.16	.05
	Seeking of group support by council	.25	.001
Intensity of group members' activity	Extent of Pluralist role orientation	.21	.01
	Seeking of group support by council	.18	.01
Political communications to policy-makers	Extent of Pluralist role orientation	.31	.001
	Seeking of group support by council	.23	.001
Group activity in elections	Extent of Pluralist role orientation	.30	.001
	Seeking of group support by council	.25	.001
Internal Consistency of Variables in Translation Process			
Relation Between:			
Number of active groups and intensity of group members' activity		.18	.01
Number of active groups and political communications to policy-makers		.24	.001
Number of active groups and group activities in elections		.15	.05
Intensity of group members' activity and political communications		.12	(NS)
Intensity of group members' activity and group activities in elections		.36	.001
Political communications to policy-makers and group activities in elections		.22	.01

Table 7–2 (continued)
Relation Between Political Translation Process and Political Conversion Process

	Correlation (Kendall's Tau B)	Significance
Internal Consistency of Variables in Conversion Process		
Relation between extent of Pluralist role orientation and seeking of group support by council	.37	.001

primarily on the objective needs of a city and council orientations toward spending.

2. Spending on amenities should rise with positive orientations toward groups, regardless of other environmental or organizational characteristics of the community.
3. Planning expenditures have no direct relation to group activities: these expenditures depend primarily on a city's developmental stage.

These expectations stem from our interpretation of the literature on political development in American communities, and more specifically, from Robert Eyestone's work.[20] General expenditures depend on a variety of factors, of which the ability of citizens to pay for new services and the objective needs of a city at a given point in time are probably the most important. Thus for a core city, most of whose high-status citizens have long since left for the suburbs, we expect high demands for expenditures coupled with a low resource base. In contrast, for a fringe community which has not yet undergone the pangs of rapid growth and even more traumatic demands for new services, there is a moderate resource base and low demands. An intermediate case might be a developing suburb which is experiencing rapid industrial and residential growth. This sort of community can meet expanding needs for new services with a potentially fecund source of taxation,

---

20 See Eyestone, *The Threads of Public Policy,* for an exhaustive discussion of the differing resources, demands, and policy preferences of councilmen in three different types of communities.

in terms of both residential wealth and taxable industrial property.

Per capita expenditure levels, in short, do not depend primarily on political demands. They depend on what Eyestone calls "resource capabilities," or the relationship between objective resources and the willingness of policy-makers to spend available revenues, within the context of the developmental stage of the community in question. The willingness of policy-makers to spend community resources may depend, in turn, on their stance toward community organizations, but we cannot assume this is the case without more empirical study. The political translation process—at least in terms of group activity—is probably not relevant to the final level of expenditures for a given community when we take into account other factors.

The same line of reasoning applies to planning expenditures. Here the "objective facts of life" for each community are apt to be much more important for the level of spending than the pressure organized groups can bring to bear on policy-makers. Group life in a city probably has little impact on the level of spending for planning; in any case, the focus of group demands is likely to depend on which groups are active in a given city. In some communities pro-planning voices such as neighborhood associations may be loudest; in others, anti-planners such as land speculators may have the upper hand.

It is only in the case of amenities spending that we anticipate a close link between the political translation process and policy output, for two reasons. First, most of the organized groups in these cities are likely to be advocates of some amenities spending. The most frequently named influential groups are Chambers of Commerce, neighborhood associations, and service clubs, all of which favor beautification and improvement projects like parks, recreation facilities, and civic centers. There are, to be sure, a fair number of taxpayers associations and various ad hoc groups dedicated to a reduced level of spending, but these are far outnumbered by the organizations named above. In addition, there are a large number of special purpose groups like youth organizations, riding associations, golden age clubs, and art, library, and music associations, all of which are likely to request special facilities (construction of buildings, bridle or bicycle paths, the conservation of land). Their claims, of course, are sometimes mutually exclusive, and they will need to compete as well with spokesmen for increased "basic" services (health, fire, and police protection).

The second reason for expecting a close relation between the degree to which councils favor and depend on local groups and the degree to which they are willing to spend for amenities hinges on the councilman's freedom of movement in this area as opposed to the basic services area. There is relatively little argument, except in some fringe cities, about the need for sewers or well-equipped fire departments. The councilman who wishes to meet the requests and demands of his constituents, insofar as possible, probably has the most freedom of choice in those optional spending areas dealing with public amenities. Therefore, the push for increased expenditures—and the resultant group struggle—is more likely to center on optional "frills" than on "basic" services.[21]

At first glance, Table 7–3 supports all three hypotheses. There is no relationship between level of per capita expenditures and either translation variable; for planning expenditures, the relation is negative. Amenities spending, in contrast, is strongly related to council orientations and behavior toward community groups. It will be recalled, though, that in the large number of studies where political variables were found correlated with various measures of policy outputs, the relation disappeared when environmental factors were controlled.[22] Examination of the third part of the table (the relation between environment and outputs) indicates that this might be the case in the present study. Partial correlations for the crucial variables are shown in Table 7–4.

---

[21] This reasoning may apply only at a time of general economic prosperity. It will be recalled that our study was undertaken in the mid-1960s, in an area undergoing rapid growth; a replication in less prosperous times or places might yield a high correlation between group activities and lower levels of spending on these "optional" amenities. In such a time and place we might also anticipate a different constellation of active groups—i.e., antispending interests may be both more vocal and more influential.

[22] See especially Dawson and Robinson, "Inter-Party Competition"; Dye, *Politics, Economics and the Public;* Sharkansky, *Spending in the American States.*

Table 7–3
Relation Between Political Conversion Process and Policy Outputs

Variable A	Variable B	Correlation (Kendall's Tau B)	Significance
Extent of Pluralist role orientation	Expenditures*	.07	(NS)
	Amenities*	.19	.01
	Planning*	–.13	.05
Seeking of group support by council	Expenditures	.10	(NS)
	Amenities	.31	.001
	Planning	–.23	.001
Alternative Explanation I: Relation Between Translation Process and Outputs			
Number of active groups	Expenditures	.06	(NS)
	Amenities	.36	.001
	Planning	.11	(NS)
Intensity of group members' activity	Expenditures	.21	.01
	Amenities	.26	.01
	Planning	–.03	(NS)
Alternative Explanation II: Relation Between Environment and Outputs			
Population	Expenditures	.03	(NS)
	Amenities	.50	.001
	Planning	.21	.01
Percentage land in industrial use	Expenditures	.29	.001
	Amenities	.33	.001
	Planning	–.01	(NS)
Percentage high school graduates	Expenditures	–.20	.01
	Amenities	.33	.001
	Planning	–.01	(NS)
Median family income	Expenditures	–.12	(NS)
	Amenities	.08	(NS)
	Planning	.13	.05

* See text above for an explanation of these indicators.

Table 7–4
Relation Between Political Conversion Process
and Policy Outputs, Controlled for Environmental Factors

Correlation	Control	Partial Correlation
Extent of Pluralist role orientation/amenities	Population	.09
Extent of Pluralist role orientation/amenities	Industrialization	.15
Seeking of group support by council/amenities	Population	.23
Seeking of group support by council/amenities	Industrialization	.26

Note the contrast between the explanatory strength of the two variables (Pluralist role orientation and seeking of group support) when population and industrialization are controlled. Clearly *council orientations* toward groups have little independent effect on amenities spending, but *council behavior* toward such groups remains important, regardless of the size or industrial character of the city concerned. Once again a measure of potential lacks the explanatory power of a measure of behavior. The political translation process is important for at least one type of policy output —amenities expenditures—but chiefly when words or attitudes are matched by deeds.

Summary

This portion of our study is one of the few in which concrete evidence for the relevance of *political* activity to policy outputs has been demonstrated. We have found, as have others before us, that policy outcomes are heavily circumscribed by the environment in which political decisions are made. In spite of this stricture, the political conversion and translation processes have an independent effect on some public policies. The complex linkage described above can be restated in simple terms. Interest groups and city councils interact within widely different socioeconomic environments, and the way and degree to which they interact vary with these environments. In large and complex cities, groups take a more active role in the political process itself. Where groups are more active, councils are more responsive. Finally, in cities where interaction between councils and groups is friendly, public spending for amenities is frequently high.

A large part of the contrast between high-amenities-spending cities and low-amenities-spending cities can be explained by the differences in the urban environment: policy-makers spend more for amenities in large, industrial cities than in small, residential communities. But even after environmental factors are taken into account, the impact of organized group activity and, more significantly, the relations between group spokesmen and official policy-makers are important for explaining outcomes in at least one policy area, the level of amenities expenditures.

We suspect that the set of political conversion and translation variables relevant to policy outcomes is markedly larger than that explored by those who have concentrated on malapportionment, voter turnout, and party competition. If adequate measures could be developed, for example, for general citizen participation and interest in urban affairs (beyond the voting act itself), or for the quality and adequacy of press coverage of local politics, perhaps further explanation of policy outcomes by means of political variables would be possible. Similarly, much more work must be done to develop measures of political outcomes that go beyond the rank-ordering of expenditure levels. The impact of expenditures on different socioeconomic groupings is an obvious topic for such an agenda; the speed and efficiency with which policy decisions are made and implemented is another.

The finding that the political activities of interest groups do make a difference, not only for the attitudes and work of local policy-makers but for the content of public policy decisions, is an important addition to contemporary theorizing about the democratic policy-making process. Perhaps the local group is the major functional equivalent in the local nonpartisan setting to the political party or to less obvious power elites. Without comparable studies of the impact of the unorganized citizenry or the local press, we cannot, of course, answer this question. Obviously, all political actors—whether group spokesmen, media leaders, organized or unorganized citizens, or elected representatives—continue to operate in an arena limited by their environment. The basic question concerns their freedom of movement within that set of constraints.

One striking conclusion emerges from this analysis concerning the difference between what we have called the political potential and the political behavior of both citizens and policy-makers. In two crucial instances, we have found that potential activity (words, attitudes, a paper organization) carries very little weight in comparison with concrete activity (group participation in elections, council reliance on group aid in selling its ideas to the community). The mere number of organized groups is not as important as their participation in the political articulation and communication processes; the favorable orientation of councilmen toward local groups explains very little of their decision-making behavior in comparison with the degree to which they make allies of those groups. The lesson is clear for both scholars and activists: the scholar must move from a study of political attitudes and orientations to a study of political behavior, if he wishes to understand the policy-making process, and the local activist must match his words on behalf of his causes with concrete deeds, if he is to be effective.

Chapter 8

Conclusion

A Summary of Findings

We have analyzed, in some detail, the origins and implications of the interest group role orientations in 82 communities. In addition, we have presented and tested a theory which links the economic environment, the quality of group life, council/group relations, and policies in these cities.

Our analysis has been guided by one general hypothesis: the behavior of elected officials toward those who attempt to influence policy outcomes is related to their general predispositions toward the interest articulation process. In accordance with this proposition, we have classified councilmen on the basis of responses to three questions. One of these probes their attitudes toward interest group activity. The others tap both the basis for, and the extent of, their awareness of group influence on the political process.

Using the typology of interest group role orientations, we have isolated a select group of councilmen, the Pluralists (about one-quarter of our respondents), who are favorably disposed toward both interest groups and the general idea of interest articulation. We predicted that these councilmen, in contrast to Tolerants and Antagonists, would not only be more aware of a wide variety of local organizations and more accommodating to these groups (especially economic groups and spokesmen for "special interests"), but would also be more likely than others to make legislative allies with local organizations. This was the case.

The majority of councilmen do not view groups as important or indispensable to the political system. As predicted, neither the Tolerants nor the Antagonists encourage group approaches, and they do not turn to such groups for help on their own projects. They apparently believe that the council, with the advice of the city manager and city staff, is generally capable of acting in the interest of the community without actively soliciting the views of the electorate or balancing conflicting claims on public resources.

It does not seem to matter, for the behavior we are describing, whether the councilman is neutral and relatively unaware or hostile and highly aware of local organizational activity. Unless groups are both salient and valued, the political actor in the local community makes very little effort to modify his behavior on their behalf. As we have stated above, *for most councilmen, the group struggle takes place on a one-way street:* Tolerants and Antagonists either avoid this street, or drive ahead, glancing neither to the side nor into their rear-view mirrors, at the noncouncil traffic accompanying them. Their destination is the relatively insulated and apolitical councilroom, where the search for "right answers" prevails, regardless of the occasional clamor outside.

Councilman/group spokesmen relations are not explained merely by the early political socialization experiences of the actors in question. Nor does the socioeconomic background of local officials hold the key to predicting their role behavior as incumbents toward local groups. Instead contrasting interest group role orientations are associated strongly with a set of recruitment and in-council experiences that point to markedly different conceptions of the political process—conceptions we have labelled "managerial" and "political." The viewpoint at one polar extreme is the tacit assumption of many students of the political process, namely, that politics consists of a group struggle or bargaining process. The second, or "managerial," view, ironically, seems to be the most widespread among local representatives, at least in the communities we have studied. Given the finding that the vast majority of our respondents adopt the managerial view, the adequacy of the group struggle model as an explanatory device is called into question. The question then arises: What difference, in terms of the concrete behavior of councilmen and the content of policy outputs, do these contrasting approaches on the part of incumbents make?

This question can be answered at two levels of analysis: the individual legislator and the local legislative system. A knowledge of councilmen's group role orientations provides considerable capacity to predict the behavior of individual councilmen. We have discussed the tendency of Pluralists to form alliances with group spokesmen; their fellow councilmen are slow to do so. In addition, we have seen a strong contrast between Pluralists and others in (1) their willingness to bargain and compromise with other councilmen; (2) their willingness to perform "errand boy" functions for constituents, and (3) their willingness to make active efforts to sell their own views to constituents. We have also found that Pluralists prefer the representational style of Delegate or Politico to that of Trustee, and that they are more likely than others to include an interest aggregation role in their purposive orientations.

This analysis has yielded two different sets of data: information on councilmen's behavior (bargaining, seeking group alliances, performing routine tasks) and information on predispositions (the taking of aggregative roles). We are inclined to place more confidence in measures of reported behavior than in measures of predispositions as indicators of the way councilmen act. Our belief that those who utilize role analysis must attempt to bridge the gap between orientations and behavior has led us, in addition, to explore the implications of the interest group role orientation for policy outputs of councils. Thus we have also examined the ties between what we call environmental factors, the translation and conversion processes, and political outputs in local communities.

Most efforts to develop political linkage theory for the study of policy outcomes and the environment have focused on two political characteristics in cities and states: party competition and citizen interest. We have approached the question from a slightly different perspective. What is the impact of differing patterns of interest articulation and political communications on the way in which public resources are allocated by councilmen? Do the efforts of interest groups, the press, and individuals to make claims on the legislative system matter, either for the manner in which policies are made or for the substance of policy decisions?

The political translation process is important for the policy-making (conversion) process. Strong relations between the potential for competition among the citizens of contrasting environments and the "group life" of these communities have been demonstrated. Furthermore, local policy-making bodies respond to differences in magnitude in the expression of local interests. Councils in cities where a large number of groups exist and/or voice demands are likely to favor organizational activities and to seek alliances. The concrete behavior of groups in local elections and in contacting their representatives carries more weight than the sheer number of organized groups.

The size, and thus the social complexity, of the communities studied is also a determinant of the group life of the community, the efforts of councilmen to process group demands, and their desire to bring groups into the policy-making process. Group activity seems to be most effective in the largest and most industrial cities. One clear point emerges specifically in regard to the group orientations and behavior of councilmen: regardless of the size or complexity of the community, group activity in elections or in contacting councilmen (in contrast to the mere existence of the group) is the key to group influence—as measured by the tendency of councilmen to seek group help and advice.

Finally, we have found that the conversion and translation processes in regard to local organizational activity are closely related to one important policy outcome: the proportion of the local budget that goes to amenities such as parks, libraries, and recreation facilities. This relation between the conversion process (the degree to which policy-makers seek group help) and amenities spending remains strong even when size and degree of industrialization of the cities studied are taken into account.

This relation between political outcomes and the translation and conversion processes is unusual in comparison with the findings of most studies of policy outputs. Almost all research of this type indicates that political variables are statistically irrelevant to the explanation of outcomes. We have found, in contrast, that interest group activity and the response of councilmen to that activity has an independent impact on the final outcomes of the policy-making process.

A seeming paradox arises when we compare the findings of Chapter 7, which dealt with whole councils, to those of earlier chapters that focused on the individual councilman. If only about a quarter of our individual respondents are highly aware of and accommodating to local organizations, how is it that group activities have any impact on council behavior and council outputs? Are these findings contradictory? Our answer is no.

A much-simplified restatement of the main linkage found in Chapter 7 makes the point. Especially in large complex cities, groups tend to be very active in campaigns and in presenting claims. Where groups are active, councils tend to be responsive and to make allies of these groups. Further, in such instances, amenities spending is higher than in cities with a less active group universe and less responsive councilmen. These *tendency* statements do not imply, however, that community organizations are invariably active in large cities, or that all councilmen in cities where groups are active are responsive to those claims. What we have shown, we believe, is that at least two different sets of data are needed to explain group influence, or lack thereof: (1) knowledge of the group's activities (and perhaps of its internal characteristics), and (2) knowledge of the policy-maker's stance toward the group. The two are not unconnected, but neither are they invariably complementary. In addition, knowledge of the environment within which groups and policy-makers operate is helpful in assessing the group life of a community.

Questions for Further Research

At several points in our analysis, we have been forced to speculate, to make inferences from scattered data, or to accept councilmen's estimates and assessments of external actors, because we lacked firsthand information on the subject. Most of the questions in need of study require new data and supplementary research techniques. We shall discuss three such areas of inquiry.

1. An independent check of the accuracy of the picture of a generally sparse "group life" in the communities studied, which emerged from responses by city councilmen.
2. A further investigation of the consequences of the mixture of differing purposive and interest group role orientations for the stability and adaptability of the political and social systems in question.
3. An investigation of interest group role orientations of councilmen in a partisan setting.

A Check on the Low Intensity of Group Life

Nearly half our respondents named two or less local groups as influential on problems dealt with by the city council. Fewer than one-fifth of these groups are of the type usually thought of as interest articulators (e.g., merchants associations, labor unions, etc.). In fact, only 13 councilmen mentioned unions at all, and such organizations were named even less frequently in connection with local political campaigns. The most prominent role during elections seems to be played, instead, by ad hoc groupings and friends of the candidate. For the remainder of the time, civic groups like the Lions Club or neighborhood associations join a handful of community influentials, the press, and the city staff in performing what interest articulation can be perceived at the community level.

In one sense, these findings are not surprising. Sociologists have long since reported that the average level of adult participation in voluntary associations is low. Bennett Berger, who made a detailed survey in 1957 among union members who had moved from one to another of the communities studied here, reported an even lower level of participation among working-class citizens, if union membership is excluded.[1]

Yet several dozen organizations are listed by the Chambers of

---

[1] Berger, *Working Class Suburb.*

Commerce as active in most of these communities, presumably with some overlap in membership. These lists include a variety of potential political groups: unions, ethnic groups, veterans' organizations, and the League of Women Voters. We have answered the question originally set forth as our major aim—what is the impact of councilmen's differing predispositions toward groups—by demonstrating that within the same council some incumbents name no groups as influential while others name several. Nevertheless, we have no way of determining whether the small number of economic interest groups mentioned reflects:

1. A relatively low level of organizational activity aimed specifically at influencing council decisions.
2. A relatively intense effort to influence council decisions, but failure to mobilize membership support or to amass necessary information for presentation at hearings or use in personal contacts with councilmen.
3. A relatively intense effort and at least moderate skill of organizations, but resistance to influence by councilmen.

There is considerable evidence from our data that, in at least some of the cities studied, the third alternative is correct.

A sample survey of leaders and members of interest groups in several of these communities might help to round out our study, particularly if questions concerning group members' expectations of councilmen were included. We might then be able to determine whether differential access of groups to any given councilman could be attributed to varying organizational skills or whether it arose from a systematic perceptual distortion on the part of the councilman.

In short, interviews with two sets of actors in these political systems would add to our knowledge of the factors involved in group influence, by focusing at the same time on both the "self" and the "other" parts of the role relationship. Such a study might also contribute to our understanding of role conflict of the interpersonal variety by bringing to light differences or similarities in the self-expectations of councilmen vis-à-vis groups and the equivalent expectations of group leaders.[2]

Investigation of the Long-Range Consequences of a Balance of Purposive and Interest Group Role Orientations for Stability and Change of the Political and Social Systems

We have suggested, on the basis of impressionistic evidence, that a dominance by Antagonist-Directors or Antagonist-Guardians on a city council could lead to serious minority unrest and ultimate system instability, whereas a dominance of Pluralist-Ritualists could lead to a failure to find solutions other than those that emerge directly from conflicting group claims. We also implied, in Chapter 7, that a study of feedback is important, but we found no adequate indicators in our present data to enable us to include it in the analysis.

An adequate test of this inference involves formidable methodological problems. It would require the development of indices for (1) substantial minority unrest and social instability, and (2) failure to find solutions other than those which emerge from the conflict of groups. The study would need to be longitudinal, and it would be very difficult to establish the causal relations in which we are interested without a large enough number of cities to guarantee a random effect of circumstantial events. Then, too, any major change affecting all cities in the area—e.g., creation by the state legislature of new metropolitan districts, a depression—might undermine the whole effort by changing the basis for comparison. Finally, interview techniques would need to be supplemented by other observational methods such as sample surveys of

2 Neal Gross, *Explorations in Role Analysis,* conducted his study in this manner through interviews with several sets of actors involved in public education, e.g., school administrators and school board members. Zeigler and Baer, *Lobbying,* interviewed both lobbyists and state legislators in their more recent study of lobbying in four states.

constituents, use of census data, council records, and/or newspaper reports.

If such a study were to be attempted, it would entail an initial division of cities into three categories: councils with no Pluralists, councils with no Antagonists, and all others. The 81 cities studied intensively in Chapter 7 are distributed as follows:

All group roles present	20	(25%)
Pluralist-Tolerant	33	(41)
Antagonist-Tolerant	12	(15)
Pluralist-Antagonist	1	(1)
Tolerant only	15	(18)
	81	(100%)

If this pattern is relatively representative over time, there should be no problem in finding an adequate number of cities in each category.

A first set of interviews, presumably with both councilmen and a sample of constituents, would establish both the mixture of role orientations and perceptions of major problems. A second set of interviews, perhaps three to five years later, would then determine the consistency over time of the mixture of role orientations as well as changing perceptions and solutions for problems.

Criteria for the two dependent variables might include:

1. *Minority unrest and system instability*—

   unrest perceived by large numbers of councilmen and constituents;

   high incidence of recall movements, charter controversies, or other issues relating to either the continuance of the current regime or the institutional arrangements;

   outbreaks of violence, strikes, demonstrations;

   high increase in crime rate or sharp population loss (relative to other cities in area).

2. *Solution to problems*—

   relatively long time taken to reach agreement, or failure to find solutions; major issues mentioned by constituents never reach council agenda;

group origin of solutions, as opposed to staff or council origin, a large proportion of time;

objective measures of failure to solve problems—decline in resource base, physical deterioration of services and facilities in comparison with neighboring communities.

The testing procedures would thus consist of a comparison of the three types of cities, over a period of several years, in the above or similar terms. We would expect, if our inferences are correct, to find the following relations:

	City Type		
Dependent Variable	No Antagonists on Council	No Pluralists on Council	All Others
Minority Unrest			
High	−	+	±
Low	+	−	±
Solutions to Problems			
Successful	−	+	±
Unsuccessful	+	−	±

The anticipated relations are, briefly, a relatively high incidence of minority unrest in cities where no Pluralists serve on the council and a relatively high incidence of failure in solving community problems in cities where no Antagonists are councilmen.

Investigation of Interest Group Role Orientations in Partisan Settings

We have found that many Antagonists and Tolerants maintain what is at base a consensual view of community politics: one we have labelled the managerial approach. In this context, interest group activity is believed to be irrelevant or disruptive. Many Pluralists esteem groups for performing both interest articulation and interest aggregation activities, and Pluralists themselves perform interest aggregation roles as part of their purposive orientations. We have also suggested that one reason for the overwhelming preference for the representational style of Trustee shown by both Tolerants and Antagonists is the lack of individuals or groups in the community from whom they are willing to accept guidance on constituency views. The majority of Pluralists apparently depend either on their contacts with groups or upon other sources of information on constituency wishes in taking the style of Politico or Delegate.

All of these findings need to be tested in settings where elections are partisan. In some political systems, party leaders perform interest aggregation functions that might enable Tolerants and Antagonists to choose the style of Delegate or Politico. Parties also perform some of the functions for which Pluralists esteem interest groups. In partisan communities, parties might replace both interest groups and incumbent councilmen as recruitment agents and sources of electoral support via slates. The degree to which these phenomena might be observed would probably vary with the degree of two-party competition in the community. It might also vary with the autonomy of the local party organizations in relation to state and national leadership.

On the other hand, it is entirely possible that at the local level the dichotomy between partisan and nonpartisan political systems is not as important as the high visibility of individual actors and the resulting personalization of roles, or the limited scope of the problems dealt with and the legal limitations on the authority of local decision-making bodies. It is possible that the suburban (managerial) ethic—the consensual model of local government—is so strong that party competition would enter into the electoral process, but not into the way in which councilmen perform their purposive tasks. Thus the party parameter may be relevant to some, but not all, of the core roles that councilmen take.

These, though, are empirical questions that are more easily tested than most of the problems discussed in this section. From the point of view of our knowledge of interest articulation and interest aggregation in small political systems, and in regard to the broad question of the applicability of the findings of the present study to other systems, they should assume a high priority on the agenda for future research.

Appendixes

Appendix A

The Research Project and the Data

This Appendix provides a brief description of the context for the analyses and interpretations reported in this and the other monographs of *The Urban Governors* series. These analyses and interpretations are grounded in or inspired by data collected at a specific "point" in time—actually over a period of some eighteen months, from January 1966 to June 1967—in a particular region of the United States. The data are "representative," therefore, in only a very limited sense. Although none of the writers of the monographs would claim greater universality for his interpretations than the data warrant, the temptation on a reader's part to forget or ignore the limitations of a clearly bounded space-time manifold is always present. The reader is entitled, therefore, to information about the setting of each study, if only for comparison with settings which are more familiar to him and which serve as his own frames of reference.

Needless to say, we cannot describe here the San Francisco Bay metropolitan region, its cities and its people, in their full richness and diversity. Clearly, only certain aspects of the environment are relevant, and this relevance must be determined by the objectives of the particular research project in which we were engaged. Before presenting the relevant context, therefore, the research project itself will be described in brief outline.

The City Council Research Project

As mentioned already in the Preface, the Project was a research and training program with as many as twelve participants working together at one time. Because the Project was intended, from the beginning, to maximize the independent research creativity of each participant, the research design had to be sufficiently flexible to permit the collection of data that would satisfy each Project member's research concerns. The monographs in this series reflect the heterogeneity of the research interests that found their way into the Project. At the same time, each researcher was necessarily limited by the Project's overall objective, which was, throughout, to gather data that would shed light on the city council as a small political decision-making group.

Our interest in the city council as a decision-making group stemmed from prior research on governance through democratic legislative processes. Political scientists have been traditionally concerned with the variety of "influences," external to the legislative body as well as internal, that shape both the legislative process and the legislative product. It was an assumption of the research that these influences could be studied more intensively in the case of small bodies than in the case of larger ones, like state legislatures or Congress, that already have been widely investigated. In particular, it was assumed that a decision-making body is both the sum of its parts and greater than the sum of its parts. Therefore, both the council as a collective unit and the councilman as an individual unit could be selected for the purposes of analysis. In the major book of this series, by Heinz Eulau and Kenneth Prewitt, the council as such serves as the unit of analysis. In the accompanying monographs, individual councilmen primarily serve as the units.

Convenience apart, the choice of the universe to be studied was dictated by the research objective. On the one hand, we needed a sufficiently large number of decision-making groups to permit systematic, quantitative, and genuinely comparative analyses at the group level. On the other hand, we needed a universe in which "influences" on the individual decision-maker and the decision-making group could be studied in a relatively uniform context. In particular, we sought a universe that provided a basic environmental, political, and legal uniformity against which city-by-city differences could be appraised. We therefore decided on a single metropolitan region in a single state in which we could assume certain constants to be present—such as *relative* economic growth, similar institutional arrangements and political patterns, identical state statutory requirements, and so on.

The price paid for this research design should be obvious. The San Francisco Bay metropolitan region is quite unlike any other metropolitan region, including even the Los Angeles metropolitan area, and it differs significantly from the Chicago, Boston, or New York metropolitan complexes. Undoubtedly, metropolitan regions, despite internal differences, can be compared as ecological units in their own right. But as our units of analysis are individual or collective decision-makers in the cities of a particular, and in many respects internally unique, region, the parameters imposed on our data by the choice of the San Francisco Bay metropolitan area recommend the greatest caution in extending, whether by analogy or inference, our findings to councils or councilmen in other metropolitan regions of other states.

All of this is not to say that particular analyses enlightened by theoretical concerns of a general nature cannot be absorbed into the growing body of political science knowledge. The City Council Research Project consciously built on previous research in other settings, seeking to identify and measure influences that have an impact on legislative processes and legislative products. The effect of the role orientations of councilmen with regard to their constituents, interest groups, or administrative officials may be compared with the effect of parallel orientations in larger legislative bodies. Their socialization and recruitment experiences, their differing styles of representational behavior, or their political strategies are probably influences not unlike those found elsewhere. Similarly, the relationships among individuals in a small group and the norms guiding their conduct may be compared with equivalent patterns in larger legislative bodies. Perceptions of the wider metropolitan environment and its problems, on the one hand, and of the city environment and its problems, on the other hand, and how these perceptions affect council behavior and outputs are of general theoretical interest. In terms of the developing theory of legislative behavior and processes, therefore, the data collected by the Project and utilized in the monographs of this series have an import that transcends the boundaries of the particular metropolitan region in which they were collected.

The Research Context

San Francisco and its neighboring eight counties have experienced an extraordinary population growth rate since the end of World War II. Many of the wartime production workers and military personnel who traveled to or through this region decided to settle here permanently in the postwar years; they and thousands of others were attracted by the moderate climate year-round, several outstanding universities, closeness to the Pacific Ocean and its related harbors, headquarters for hundreds of West Coast branches of national firms and, of course, the delightful charm of San Francisco itself. Other resources and assets exist in abundance: inviting ski resorts and redwood parks are within short driving distance; hundreds of miles of ocean lie to the immediate west; mile after mile of grape vineyards landscape the nearby Livermore and Napa valleys. All of these, linked by the vast San Francisco Bay and its famous bridges, make this one of the nation's most distinctive and popular metropolitan regions.

Larger than the state of Connecticut and almost as large as New Jersey and Massachusetts combined, this nine-county region now houses four million people; about six million more are expected by 1980. At the time of the study, 90 cities and at least 500 special districts served its residents.

As has been pointed out already, no claim can be made that the San Francisco Bay region is typical of other metropolitan areas; indeed, it differs considerably on a number of indicators. Unlike most of the other sizable metropolitan regions, the Bay region has experienced its major sustained population boom in the 1950s and 1960s. This metropolitan area is also atypical in that it has not one major central city but three—namely San

Francisco, Oakland, and San Jose. And while San Francisco continues to be the "hub" and the region's dominant city, Oakland and San Jose are rival economic and civic centers. San Jose, moreover, anticipates that its population will triple to nearly a million people in the next 20 years. Of additional interest is the fact that this region has pioneered in the creation of one of the nation's prototypes of federated urban governmental structures. Its Association of Bay Area Governments, organized in 1961, has won national attention as one of the first metropolitan councils of local governments.

Although in many respects unlike other metropolitan regions, the San Francisco Bay region resembles some in the great diversity among its cities. Omitting San Francisco proper, 1965 city populations ranged from 310 to 385,700. Population densities in 1965 ranged from 71 to 12,262 persons per square mile. The rate of population growth between 1960 and 1965 ranged from zero to 204 percent. Median family incomes ranged from $3,582 to $23,300, and percent nonwhite from 0.1 to 26.4.

Institutionally, the governments of the cities in the San Francisco Bay region are predominantly of the council-manager or council-administrator form, although some of the very small cities may rely on the chief engineer rather than on a manager or administrator. Cities may be either of the "charter" or "general law" type. Charter cities differ from general law cities in having greater control over election laws, the size of their councils, the pay of municipal officers, and tax rate limitations. General law cities have five councilmen, while charter cities may have more than this number. Among the cities included in the research, the number of councilmen per city ranged from five to thirteen.

All local officials in California, including, of course, those interviewed in the City Council Research Project, are elected under a nonpartisan system. With a few exceptions, councilmen run at large and against the entire field of candidates. In five cities there is a modified district election plan in which candidates stand in a particular district but all voters cast ballots for any candidate. Ten cities elect the mayor separately; in the remaining cities the mayor is either the candidate receiving the highest number of votes or is selected by vote of the council.

Map A–1
Bay Area Place Names

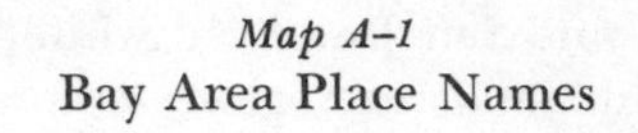

Council candidates must have been residents of the community for at least one year prior to their election. For the most part they are elected to serve two-year terms, though charter cities may vary this. Only three cities have tenure limitations. The great majority of councilmen receive no compensation for their services or, if any, only a token compensation to cover expenses. For most, the council is a part-time activity.

The powers of the city councilmen may be exercised only as a group; that is, individual councilmen have no power to act alone. The council may meet only at duly convened public meetings and at a place designated by ordinance. Council meetings must be regularly scheduled and held no less than once a month, but when council action is required between regularly scheduled meetings, the statutes allow procedures for calling special meetings. The "Brown Act," passed in 1953 and in effect during the time our interviewing took place, requires all council meetings to be public and publicized, except for executive sessions on personnel matters.

The Data Bases

Five sets of data were generated or systematized by the Project. First, data from the U.S. Census of Population for 1960 and estimates for 1965 served a variety of analytical purposes. Because the data included in the census and its categories are well known, we need not say more about this data set. Specific uses made of census data and the rationale for such uses are explained in each monograph wherever appropriate. All members of the research team were involved in readying the census data for analysis.

Second, data concerning city income, resources, and expenditures were available in the State Controller's *Annual Report of Financial Transactions Concerning Cities of California*. These reports include breakdowns suitable for comparative anlaysis of Bay region cities for the year 1958–1959 through 1965–1966. How the measures derived from this data set were handled is described in appropriate places of the monograph series where the data are used. Robert Eyestone was largely responsible for preparing this data set.

Third, local election data over a ten-year period, 1956 through 1966, were collected by Gordon Black, with the collaboration of Willis D. Hawley at the Institute of Governmental Studies, University of California, Berkeley. These data were obtained directly from the various cities, and they include the voting returns for each of five elections in each city, the registration figures for the city at each election period, and a variety of facts about individual candidates. These facts include incumbency, partisan affiliation, length of time in office, and the manner in which the incumbents gained office, whether by appointment or by election. A number of measures were constructed from these data, including measures of competition, partisan composition, voluntary retirement, forced turnover, and so forth. Descriptions of these measures can be found in the monographs that employ them.

Fourth and fifth, the core of the data on which the analyses are based come from interviews with city councilmen or from self-administered questionnaires filled out by councilmen. These two data sets need more detailed exposition.

1. Interview Data

With the exception of a city incorporated while the field work was under way (Yountville) and the city of San Francisco itself, interviews were sought with 488 city councilmen holding office in all the other 89 cities of the San Francisco Bay area. Although interviews were held with some members of the board of supervisors of the city-county of San Francisco, these interviews are not used in this and the other monographs owing to the city's unique governmental structure and the highly professionalized nature of its legislative body.

In two of the 89 cities (Millbrae and Emeryville), all councilmen refused to be interviewed. In the remaining 87 cities, 435 incumbent councilmen were interviewed. This constitutes 89 percent of the total population or 91 percent of the councilmen from the 87 cities that cooperated in the study. The interviews were conducted by members of the research team or by professional interviewers. Most of the respondents were interviewed in their homes, places of business, or city hall offices. All of them had been invited to visit the Stanford campus, and a small number accepted the invitation and were interviewed there.

Although the bulk of the interviewing was done between January and April 1966, some councilmen were interviewed as late as June 1967. The interview schedule was an extensive one. It included some 165 major open-end questions and additional probes, ranging over a wide variety of topics. Every effort was made to record verbatim the comments which most councilmen supplied in abundance. The interviews lasted from two to five hours or longer and averaged about three hours. Parts of the interview schedule were pretested as early as 1962 and as late as 1965, with councilmen in the metropolitan region itself and with councilmen in a neighboring county.

The interview data were coded by members of the research team responsible for particular analyses. The coded data were recorded on 17 machine-readable storage cards. They will be made available for secondary analysis on tape in due time, upon completion of all studies in *The Urban Governors* series.

2. Questionnaire

In addition to the interview, each respondent was asked to fill out a questionnaire made up of closed questions. These included a set of 35 check-list items, two pages of biographical items, and a set of 58 agree-disagree attitude items. The strategy of self-administered questionnaires was dictated by the length of the interview, for, in spite of its length, the data needs of the team members could not be satisfied by the interview instrument alone. The questionnaires were left with each respondent by the interviewer. If at all possible, interviewers were instructed to have the questionnaires filled out by the respondent immediately upon completion of the interview, but the length of the interview often did not permit this, and respondents were then asked to return the questionnaires by mail. As a result, there was some loss of potential data because councilmen neglected to return the completed forms. Nevertheless, of the 435 councilmen who were interviewed, 365, or 84 percent, completed the questionnaires. Perhaps the greatest strategic mistake in this procedure was our failure to administer the biographical and demographic background items as part of the interview.

The Sample: A Brief Profile

Although individual demographic data for all 435 councilmen who were interviewed are not available, our sample of 365 for which the data are at hand is probably representative. We shall present, therefore, a brief profile of these respondents.

On the average, San Francisco Bay region councilmen are well educated and have comfortable incomes (see Figure A–1). They are engaged in either business or professional activities. Table A–1 shows the principal lines of work of those council members who are not retired or housewives.

Councilmen in the Bay region are predominantly middle-aged, usually coming to the council while in their 40s or around 50 years of age. The turnover rate of city councilman positions is relatively high, with only a few members staying in office for more than three or four terms. The data in Figure A–1 show that close to 70 percent of the councilmen came into office for the first time within the previous five years. In open-end conversations with councilmen, many responded that they looked upon the job as a community service, as something that should be rotated among the local activists like themselves.

Table A–1
Principal Employment of City Councilmen
(of Employed Councilmen) (N = 351)

Manufacturing, utilities	22%
Banking, insurance, accountancy	21
Business, commerce, real estate	13
Lawyer	10
Construction, trucking	16
Civil Servant, public administration	14
Agriculture	4
	100%

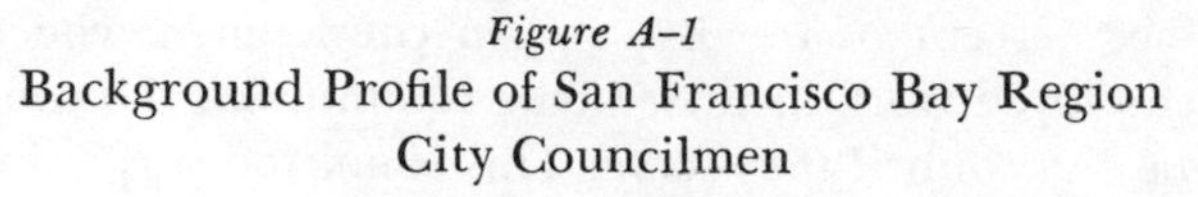

Figure A–1
Background Profile of San Francisco Bay Region City Councilmen

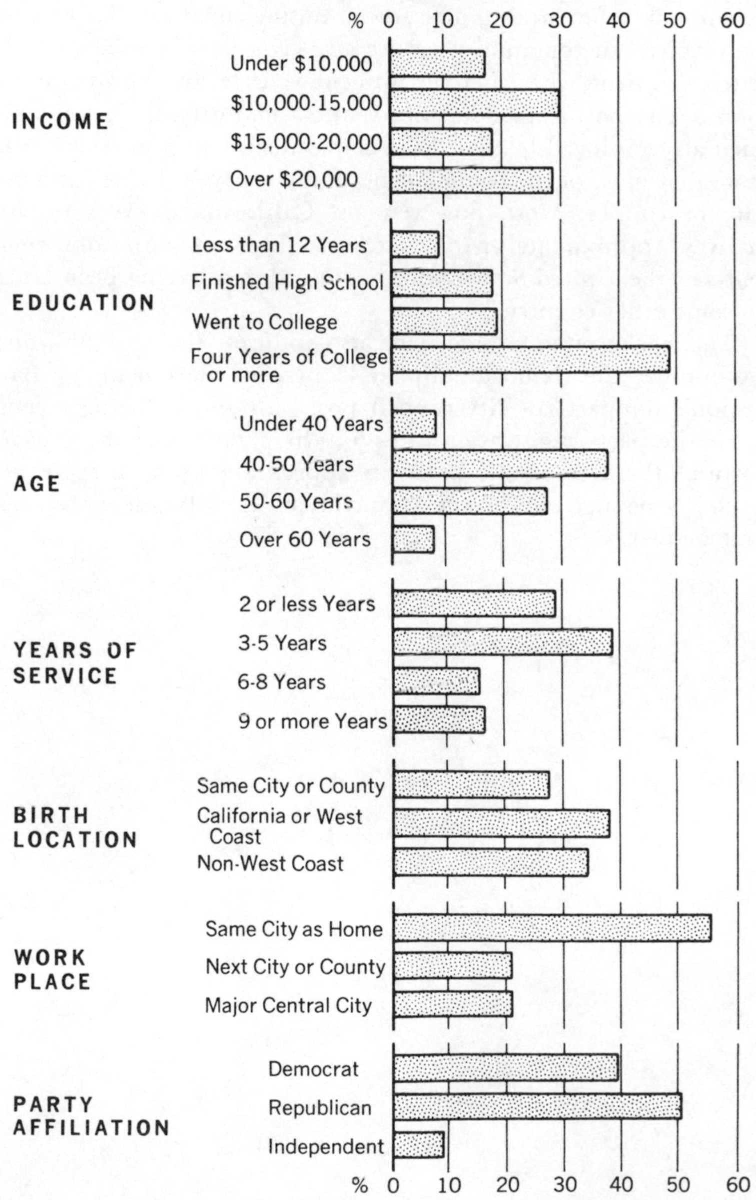

Fifty-six percent of the Bay region councilmen who are currently employed work in their home community, the community on whose city council they serve. This is not too surprising, for it is customary for local "home town" businessmen and lawyers to be involved in community service and civic undertakings, which often constitute the chief recruitment vehicle for the identification of city political leadership. While a majority of the councilmen are employed in their local communities, it is instructive to note that most of the councilmen are not natives of their present city or county. Most, however, are California or West Coast natives. Approximately a third moved to the Bay region from other parts of the United States, with about a dozen having been born in some other country.

The background profile data also indicate that Republicans outnumber the Democrats by an 11 percent margin in the Bay region's nonpartisan city council posts, although during recent years the party registration rates for the general electorate have favored the Democratic party in approximately a three-to-two ratio. Nine percent of the councilmen identify themselves as Independents.

Appendix B

Bibliographic Essay on Approaches to the Study of Interest Groups and Local Politics

No study, least of all the present one, is without antecedents. We have cited work on a range of subjects including legislative behavior, community power, political recruitment, and policy outputs. Two traditions, however, have been of central importance for our own analysis. These are: (1) past studies aimed at building middle-range theory which could handle interest group-legislative relations; and (2) studies of local government and suburbia which expanded the traditional legal-institutional focus to include relations between a range of official and unofficial actors, or which took into account the impact of general community norms on the behavior of local officials.

Approaches to Interest Group-Legislative Relations

Since the publication of David Truman's *The Governmental Process* (New York: Alfred A. Knopf, 1951), several promising approaches to the study of interest groups have been developed. We consider, briefly, four such models: group theory as described by Truman and others; the communications model utilized by Lester Milbrath; the interaction model by Harmon Zeigler and

Michael Baer; and the role analysis approach to the legislative system developed by Wahlke and his associates.

Truman conceives of the political process as a competition between social groups, the object of which is the acquisition of values. Man can acquire values only through interaction with others in groups. Targets for groups include political institutions; the success of a given group will depend largely upon *access* to these institutions. Access in turn depends on tactical skills and internal characteristics like organizational structure and cohesion. The outcome of the group struggle on specific issues will depend on the relative strength of the contenders.

Truman does not conclude his formulation at this point. He goes on to acknowledge not only the relevance of the group affiliations of legislators and administrators, but also the importance of the "influence of office." The legislature itself is viewed as a "group which enters into the group process with other groups." The problem in utilizing Truman's version of group theory is now apparent: group theory, in its most narrow sense, cannot account for all relevant factors. For example, possible cross-pressures arising from a legislator's membership in both the "legislative group" and an outside organization are not simply resolved in terms of the relative frequency of his interaction in each group. Relations between individual legislators and outside groups are not entirely idiosyncratic. Reference is generally made, by the legislator, to both institutional requirements and the expectations of others. Truman realizes this, and draws on role theory in discussing both internal and external norms associated with official status. If group theory is broadened to this degree—drawing on external formulations to fill conceptual gaps and blurring all distinction between the "pressure group" and the "pressured"—it becomes cumbersome for hypothesis building. How are group-based variables related to those that arise from the role expectations of legislators not attributable to their associations with outside groups? For example, is the leadership skill of a group more or less important than informal legislative norms that might conflict with group requests? Are claims made on a legislative actor by fellow incumbents more or less important than those made by groups outside the legislature?

Group theory is probably most useful in pointing out the relevant variables for dealing with the group side of interest group-legislator relations and weakest in dealing with the legislator's predispositions and orientations. It cannot cope with the question of individual influence (e.g., Einstein writing to the President), since it is assumed that all influence is based on group affiliations. For a study dealing with the local community this is a question which must be left open to testing.

Another model which partially overcomes the objections to Truman's theory is Lester Milbrath's communications model (*The Washington Lobbyists,* Chicago: Rand McNally, 1963). The model of government as a communication process, with lobbying as one aspect of that process, can take into account both horizontal and vertical flows of communications between legislators and a variety of groups and individuals inside and outside the legislature. Its major weakness, for present purposes, is its extreme generality or universality. It becomes difficult to apply it to a highly specific process like group efforts to influence legislation.

Another problem with this model is its failure to include variables associated with the *pre*-communication phase of the legislative process. Furthermore, if relations between a legislator and two sets of potential communicators give rise to role conflict on the part of the legislator, it is difficult to see how the communications model can handle this without drawing on decision-making or role theory. There is no objection to an eclectic approach. The question is simply which model is most easily applicable to a specific problem. In this instance role theory appears to be more appropriate.

Yet another approach (and one similar in some ways to Milbrath's) is Harmon Zeigler and Michael Baer's study of lobbying as an interaction process (*Lobbying: Interaction and Influence in American State Legislatures,* Belmont, Calif.: Wadsworth Publishing Company, 1969). Zeigler and Baer avoid one major objection to Milbrath's theory by incorporating into their own model the perceptual and attitudinal premises upon which legislators and lobbyists act. They achieve a major breakthrough with their systematic application of social-psychological theory to political problems and their attempt to explain political phenomena by that theory. Even more important, their study represents one of a handful of attempts to study a single political arena with data obtained from the perspective of more than one set of actors.

Despite its theoretical promise and its obvious advantages, we have not adopted the interaction approach for this study. Two reasons entered into this decision. First, interaction theory does not lend itself to dealing with legislative *norms,* and because of this, there is no convenient way to deal with role conflict. If a conflict between a legislator's (self-perceived) obligation to his fellow-legislators and his obligation to various constituents arises, there seems no systematic way to deal with the phenomena, in the context of interaction analysis, except by individualistic psychological mechanisms of misperception and compartmentalization. There is no way in which the legislator-lobbyist relationship can be easily imbedded into the *whole* local legislative process.

The fourth approach to the study of interest groups, and the one to which the present study is most indebted, is the combination of role analysis and systems theory developed by John Wahlke and associates in their study of legislative systems in four states (*The Legislative System: Explorations in Legislative Behavior,* New York: John Wiley and Sons, 1962). Our reasons for adopting this approach are explained in Chapter 1 and 2.

Studies of Suburbia and Local Government

Two major problems arose in formulating our theory and in analyzing our data. The first was that of making the choice of an appropriate theoretical framework. The second was in applying and adapting this orientation to the research site of the local nonpartisan political system. This task requires a discussion of at least some of the previous work most pertinent to the study of local communities.

Scott Greer, in *The Emerging City* (New York: The Free Press, 1962), pictures the city as "one macro-cosmic role system in which categories of groups perform the various tasks necessary for the totality to stay alive and healthy" (pp. 39–40). Government is assigned the role of mediator and enforcer, and the relation between official bodies and interest groups is similar to that described by theorists of the group struggle.

Yet, Greer points out, one consequence of metropolitan fragmentation is the separation of the place of work from the place of residence. This results in the inability or unwillingness of those most affected by decisions to make their weight felt. The central city government makes decisions affecting the corporations within its boundaries; the corporations' executive and white-collar employees live elsewhere, and their children swell the ranks of suburban schools whose authorities cannot tax the corporations for support. The residents of the city are primarily working-class groups with a low rate of political participation and some small businessmen. These small businessmen, along with party leaders, fill the power vacuum in the city. In the meantime, corporate businessmen, who feel little personal stake in their work place, pour their energies into the "toy government of suburbia." Neither the stand-pat governments of minimum-tax suburbs nor the near-bankrupt central city governments are able to provide essential services or to solve common problems because those with the greatest stake in the decisions of each are apathetic or have turned their attention elsewhere.

Robert Wood (*Suburbia: Its People and Their Politics,* Boston: Houghton Mifflin Co., 1959) analyzes the government of the suburbs in ideological terms. The unique qualities of suburban politics are the general reaction against partisan activity, general refusal to recognize the possibility of enduring cleavages, and disapproval of group competition as a means for settling public disputes. Thus, in casting his vote, the suburbanite is expected to seek a consensus, but with political parties banished from the scene and the citizen himself unwilling to assume the demanding role postulated by the suburban ethos, the local bureaucracy makes the decisions "by default." Suburban man may ultimately become quite apolitical.

Both Wood and Greer thus call into question, at least by implication, the adequacy of the group struggle model in explaining community political systems. If Wood is correct, the consensual model in suburbia precludes such a struggle. If Greer is right (and the two analyses are not contradictory but complementary), the bifurcation of power between suburb and central city implies that the natural contenders will seldom confront each other in the same political arena.

Two other studies of suburbia are particularly interesting in that they deal with two of the communities on which the present report is based. Robert Carmody ("An Island in Suburbia: The Study of an Upperclass Residential Community Resisting the Impact of Urbanization," unpublished MA thesis, Stanford University, 1959) studied an upper-class residential suburb. Bennett Berger (*Working Class Suburb: A Study of Auto Workers in Suburbia,* Berkeley: University of California Press, 1960) interviewed a sample of 100 auto workers who had moved from an industrial city (also one of our 82 cities) to a blue-collar suburb when the firm employing them had relocated.

Carmody confirms Wood's model through his study of conflict between the internalized values of city councilmen (a determination to keep the community as it is) with the values of school board members, who represent newer, younger, and less affluent residents. The potential for social and political conflict existed in this suburb, but each decision-making unit apparently avoided it by operating on behalf of a limited segment of the community. Requests that implied any need for a change in general values were ignored by the council as contrary to the good of the community.

Berger's main theme is the divergence of working-class behavior from the pattern of an intense social life, return to religion, adoption of middle-class tastes, change in party affiliation, and avid participation in voluntary associations attributed to suburbia by William Whyte (*The Organization Man,* New York: Simon and Schuster, 1956) and others. Berger offers the hypothesis that for these working-class residents suburbia is the end of the road, rather than a transient place on the path upward. His most important finding, for our purposes, is that in the suburb that he studies both interest in politics and membership in interest groups are considerably lower than the national average. He alerts us against the facile assumption that the residential-industrial character of communities can be used to account, by itself, for the pattern of interest articulation or the dominant norms of local government.

A variety of explanations have been offered for differing interest articulation patterns in the local community. Robert Salisbury ("St. Louis Politics: Relations Among Interests, Parties and Governmental Structure," *Western Political Quarterly* 13 [1960]: 498–507) suggests that the structure of local government may in itself shape the nature and scope of political conflict. He finds two broad configurations of interests: those oriented to bread-and-butter issues, and those interested in broader policies like economic growth. These groups operate relatively independently within the political parties as well as in regard to government agencies. The one group focuses its activity on the office of mayor while the other works with county officials.

Charles Liebman ("Electorates, Interest Groups and Local Government Policy," *American Behavioral Scientist* 5 [1961]: 8–11) presents a variant on the same theme, distinguishing "personnel oriented" interest groups from "policy oriented" interest groups. The former (ethnic and religious groups) are mainly concerned with elections, while the latter (primarily economic groups) exchange the electoral arena for the later stages of policy-making. He suggests that as the personnel-oriented groups begin to gain their objectives, the newly elected officials become a channel of access to the policy-making process and the group itself then becomes policy oriented.

No study of community decision-making can ignore either the rich theoretical insights or the findings of Robert Dahl's study of New Haven (*Who Governs? Democracy and Power in an American City,* Chicago: University of Chicago Press, 1956) or Edward Banfield's of Chicago (*Political Influence,* New York: The Free Press, 1961). Both of these analyses sounded the death knell for the universal applicability of a model of monolithic "power elites" in local communities. Both highlight the diversity of components entering into the decision-making process and the shifting nature of alignments supporting or opposing policy issues.

At the same time, the "pluralist" school has come under increasing attack from a number of sources. William Gamson ("Stable Unrepresentation in American Society," *American Be-*

havioral Scientist 12 [1968]: 15–21) has argued, for example, that the American system normally operates to exclude a great many incipient claimants. His alternative to the pluralist model is one of "stable unrepresentation," which depends on the "*consequences* of discouraging the translation of grievances into political demands which can be effectively pursued through political action." A major mechanism for this exclusion of claimants is "incrementalism"—the determination of major allocations by a large number of small, compartmentalized, and seemingly insignificant decisions. Peter Bachrach and Morton Baratz ("Two Faces of Power," *American Political Science Review* 56 [1962]: 947–953) take an even stronger position, emphasizing the frequency with which major policy questions are deliberately prevented, by controlling elites, from reaching the decision-making arena itself.

These questions can only be answered by reference to empirical data. It is entirely possible that several appropriate models of community decision-making (or nondecision-making) can be developed to fit different types of communities. Oliver Williams and associates (*Suburban Differences and Metropolitan Policies: A Philadelphia Story*, Philadelphia: University of Pennsylvania Press, 1965) found that economic outputs varied with the demographic characteristics of Philadelphia suburbs. Walter T. Martin ("The Structuring of Social Relationships Engendered by Suburban Residence," *American Sociological Review* 21 [1956]: 446–453) has discussed the unique characteristics of commuter suburbs. Both Bennett Berger and Herbert J. Gans (*The Levittowners: Ways of Life and Politics in a New Suburban Community*, New York: Random House, 1967) have highlighted the importance of the class and ethnic base of still other suburbs. It would not be surprising to find that the Dahl model fits one set of communities while the Gamson-Bachrach-Baratz model fits another.

Appendix C

Construction of the Typology of Interest Group Role Orientations

The typology of councilmen's interest group role orientations was constructed on the basis of three variables: councilmen's attitudes toward interest groups; the extent to which influential groups are perceived; and level of sophistication with regard to the group universe.

Attitude

A councilman's role orientation toward interest groups depends, in large part, on his attitude toward groups, i.e., on the way he evaluates group activity. A threefold attitudinal classification was made of responses to the question: "How do you feel about efforts of groups to make their views known to you and seek your support?" Councilmen were divided into those who:

1. *esteem* groups (believe that groups are useful in providing information, in mobilizing support, in clarifying issues);
2. are *neutral* toward groups (believe that groups are neither useful nor harmful);

3. *reject* groups (believe that groups are harmful, disruptive, time-wasting, selfish).

Perception

A classification of councilmen solely on the basis of attitudes is not likely to be a useful predictor of role behavior unless variations in the salience of local groups for individual councilmen are also taken into account. One must at least be aware of a potential ally or enemy within the political system to be motivated to interact with him, or to adjust one's behavior to his expectations. This is equally true whether the behavioral adjustment is based on negative or positive affect. The extent of a councilman's perception of interest groups, as indicated by the number of groups he *names as influential,* can serve as a first approximation of the salience of groups for him. Councilmen were divided into two groups on the basis of responses to the question, "Speaking of groups or organizations here in (city) which are active in community affairs and sometimes appear before the council—which would you say are the most influential?":

1. Those who *perceive one group or none* (name 0–1 groups as influential in their community).
2. Those who *perceive two groups or more* (name 2 or more influential groups).

The criterion for this distinction can be defended on both theoretical and pragmatic grounds. The councilman who names only one group probably differs in important respects from those who name two or more. He may be mentioning his major reference group (e.g., the union local from which he takes most of his cues) without being aware of the activities of other organizations in the community. This is much less likely to be true of the respondent who mentions two groups. In addition, it is desirable to set the cut-off point as low as possible in order to allow for differences in the way that councilmen interpret the word "influential" and variations in the complexity of the group universe in different communities.

Group Sophistication

Perception is not, by itself, an adequate measure of salience. It does not distinguish between councilmen who perceive groups as potential interest articulators and councilmen who are unaware of the capacity of groups to perform this input function. If the assumption is made that significantly different role orientations and role behavior may be observed between those who conceive of the political system as interest-based, and who thus perceive groups as structures performing articulation functions, and those who perceive groups as nothing more than a number of individuals with certain desirable or undesirable traits, an additional variable to indicate this difference must be included in a typology of role orientations.

We have termed those who perceive groups as interest articulators in a political system "sophisticated" in regard to the group universe. The measure used is perception of components of group influence, in response to the question, "What would you say makes these groups so influential—what are the main reasons for their influence?" Councilmen were classified as:

1. *sophisticated,* if they mention objective strength (size, voting power, wealth) and/or "stake in society" as components of group influence;
2. *unsophisticated,* if they confine themselves to a discussion of respect variables—honesty, intelligence, common sense, etc.

We would expect an "unsophisticated" councilman to adopt an orientation toward groups bordering on indifference or neutrality—as is probably the case with councilmen who perceive few or no groups. In contrast, councilmen with a more active orientation would demonstrate a greater degree of either perception or group sophistication.

As indicated in Chapter 2, three types of councilmen were distinguished on the basis of these three variables:

1. *Pluralists*: those who esteem groups, who perceive many groups, and who are relatively sophisticated in regard to the group universe;
2. *Tolerants*: (a) those who are neutral toward groups, regardless of perception or sophistication; (b) those who esteem or reject groups but demonstrate both a low level of perception and sophistication; (c) those who esteem groups but are either unsophisticated or low perceivers;
3. *Antagonists*: those who reject groups and demonstrate high perception and/or sophistication.

The distribution of our respondents is reported in Chapter 2.

Appendix D

*Partial Correlations for Variables Discussed in Chapter 7**

Variable A	Variable B	Correlation	Control Variable	Partial Correlation
Population	Number of active groups	.52	Percentage land in industrial use	.49
	Intensity of group members' activity	.27	Percentage land in industrial use	.19
	Political communications of groups	.27	Percentage land in industrial use	.22
			Percentage high school graduates	.26
			Median family income	.26
	Group activity in elections	.19	Percentage land in industrial use	.11
			Percentage high school graduates	.19
			Median family income	.19
Percentage land in industrial use	Number of active groups	.20	Population	.02
	Intensity of group members' activity	.28	Population	.20
			Median family income	.28

Variable A	Variable B	Correlation	Control Variable	Partial Correlation
	Political communications of groups	.18	Population	.09
	Group activity in elections	.25	Population	.20
Percentage high school graduates	Number of active groups	.03	Population	−.02
	Intensity of group members' activity	−.02	Population	−.05
	Political communications of groups	.17	Population	.15
			Median family income	.05
	Group activity in elections	.04	Population	.02
Median family income	Number of active groups	.05	Population	.00
	Intensity of group members' activity	−.08	Population	−.11
	Political communications of groups	.19	Population	.17
			Percentage high school graduates	.10
	Group activity in elections	.05	Population	.03
Number of active groups	Extent of Pluralist role orientation	.16	Population	.05
	Seeking of group support by council	.25	Population	.17
Intensity of group members' activity	Extent of Pluralist role orientation	.21	Population	.16
	Seeking of group support by council	.18	Population	.13
Political communications of groups	Extent of Pluralist role orientation	.31	Population	.27
	Seeking of group support by council	.23	Population	.18
Group activity in elections	Extent of Pluralist role orientation	.30	Population	.27
	Seeking of group support by council	.25	Population	.22

Variable A	Variable B	Correlation	Control Variable	Partial Correlation
Extent of Pluralist role orientation	Amenities as percentage of expenditures	.19	Population	.09
			Percentage land in industrial use	.15
			Number of active groups	.14
			Intensity of group activity	.14
Seeking of group support by council	Amenities	.31	Population	.23
			Percentage land in industrial use	.26
			Number of active groups	.24
			Intensity of group members' activity	.28
Number of active groups	Amenities	.36	Population	.15
			Extent of Pluralist orientation	.34
			Seeking of group support by council	.31
Intensity of group members' activity	Amenities	.26	Population	.22
			Extent of Pluralist orientation	.23
			Seeking of group support by council	.22
Population	Amenities	.50	Number of active groups	.39
			Intensity of group members' activity	.46
			Extent of Pluralist orientation	.48
			Seeking of group support by council	.46

*Our selection of "control variables" was guided by the strength of the relationship between those variables and Variables A and B in the Table. We have not presented all possible controls, since many are clearly not important. For example, we have controlled for population in almost every instance, because population is strongly related to most variables; we have not controlled for median family income or percentage of high school graduates, in contrast, because the initial relations were unimpressive for these variables.

Index